Actionable Feedback to PK–12 Teachers

Actionable Feedback to PK–12 Teachers

Edited by
Alyson L. Lavigne
Mary Lynne Derrington

ROWMAN & LITTLEFIELD
Lanham • Boulder • New York • London

Published by Rowman & Littlefield
An imprint of The Rowman & Littlefield Publishing Group, Inc.
4501 Forbes Boulevard, Suite 200, Lanham, Maryland 20706
www.rowman.com

86-90 Paul Street, London EC2A 4NE, United Kingdom

Copyright © 2023 by Alyson L. Lavigne and Mary Lynne Derrington

All rights reserved. No part of this book may be reproduced in any form or by any electronic or mechanical means, including information storage and retrieval systems, without written permission from the publisher, except by a reviewer who may quote passages in a review.

British Library Cataloguing in Publication Information Available

Library of Congress Cataloging-in-Publication Data

Names: Lavigne, Alyson Leah, editor. | Derrington, Mary Lynne, editor.
Title: Actionable feedback to PK–12 teachers / edited by Alyson L. Lavigne, Mary Lynne Derrington.
Description: Lanham, Maryland : Rowman & Littlefield, 2023. | Series: Bridging theory and practice | Includes bibliographical references and index. | Summary: "This text offers feedback strategies to teacher supervisors. Readers will acquire knowledge, resources, and activities leading to feedback that is specific, sensitive to context and content, and informed by best practice"—Provided by publisher.
Identifiers: LCCN 2022047331 (print) | LCCN 2022047332 (ebook) | ISBN 9781475866186 (cloth) | ISBN 9781475866193 (paperback) | ISBN 9781475866209 (epub)
Subjects: LCSH: Teachers—Rating of. | Teaching—Evaluation. | Effective teaching. | Observation (Educational method) | Feedback (Psychology)
Classification: LCC LB2838 .A29 2023 (print) | LCC LB2838 (ebook) | DDC 371.14/4—dc23/eng/20221129
LC record available at https://lccn.loc.gov/2022047331
LC ebook record available at https://lccn.loc.gov/2022047332

Contents

ACKNOWLEDGMENTS   vii
SERIES EDITOR'S INTRODUCTION   1
EDITORS' INTRODUCTION   7

SECTION I: The Big Picture of Supervision and Feedback

CHAPTER 1. PROMISING SUPERVISORY THEORIES AND STRATEGIES FOR INSTRUCTIONAL IMPROVEMENT   11
Helen M. Hazi

CHAPTER 2. PROVIDING FEEDBACK FOR EVALUATION AND PROFESSIONAL LEARNING   23
Monica Anthony, Wyatt Hall, Michael W. Krell, and Colleen Moore Eccles

CHAPTER 3. DEVELOPMENTAL AND DIFFERENTIATED FEEDBACK FOR EDUCATORS   35
Ellie Drago-Severson and Jessica Blum-DeStefano

CHAPTER 4. A STRATEGIC HUMAN RESOURCE ORIENTATION TO TEACHER SUPERVISION   49
Melissa Tuytens, Eva Vekeman, and Geert Devos

CHAPTER 5. THE USE OF VIDEO ANALYSIS IN SUPERVISION   63
Valerie Johnson and Benterah C. Morton

CHAPTER 6. CULTURALLY RESPONSIVE INSTRUCTIONAL SUPERVISION: (RE)ENVISIONING FEEDBACK FOR EQUITABLE CHANGE   75
Ian M. Mette, Dwayne Ray Cormier, and Yanira Oliveras-Ortiz

CHAPTER 7. FEEDBACK TO IMPROVE CULTURALLY RESPONSIVE INSTRUCTION   89
Maika Yeigh

SECTION II: Specific Applications of Feedback

CHAPTER 8. BUILDING LEADERSHIP CONTENT KNOWLEDGE TO SUPERVISE TEACHERS IN STEM DISCIPLINES   107
Sarah Quebec Fuentes, Jo Beth Jimerson, and Mark A. Bloom

CHAPTER 9. RESEARCH-BASED SUPERVISION AND FEEDBACK PRACTICES IN LITERACY INSTRUCTION   123
Janice A. Dole, Parker C. Fawson, and D. Ray Reutzel

CHAPTER 10. LEADERSHIP CONTENT KNOWLEDGE FOR EARLY CHILDHOOD: MAKING FEEDBACK MEANINGFUL   135
Maria Boeke Mongillo and Kristine Reed Woleck

CHAPTER 11. SUPERVISION AND OBSERVATION IN THE GIFTED EDUCATION CLASSROOM   149
Keri M. Guilbault, Kimberley L. Chandler, and Sarah A. Caroleo

CHAPTER 12. THE VALUE AND NECESSITY OF DIFFERENTIATION IN OBSERVATION AND FEEDBACK FOR CAREER AND TECHNICAL EDUCATION TEACHERS   163
Lee Westberry and Sonya Addison-Stewart

CHAPTER 13. SUPERVISING IN A VIRTUAL SCHOOL CONTEXT   177
Jeana Partin and Mary Lynne Derrington

THEMES AND FUTURE DIRECTIONS   191
INDEX   193
ABOUT THE CONTRIBUTORS   197

Acknowledgments

We would like to extend our gratitude to Kelsey Lamb, who helped review chapters and contributions for formatting and style. We would also like to thank Ryan Rarick and Dan Hansen for compiling a stellar index. Finally, we thank those who provided initial feedback on our book proposal that resulted in the exciting edited series text that we present here.

Series Editor's Introduction

Why a new book series on school leadership, and what does this particular series have to offer among the many fine books already published in the field of school and educational leadership?

Research over the past decade has confirmed what many educators, policy makers, think tanks, and others viscerally knew—that leadership makes a difference for a host of dependent variables, including the most important one: student achievement. Additional research is needed, however, to more fully refine and uncover how, in fact, school leaders make a difference in a host of other areas. The answers to additional research questions will offer further legitimacy and draw greater attention to the field of educational leadership. The questions (which can possibly prompt potential authors to submit a book proposal) include the following, among others:

- What does the continuing increased accountability and high-stakes testing have on teacher morale, principal self-efficacy, and student achievement?
- What additional information do we need about systems thinking and its relationship to school leadership?
- What are the specific gender differences as related to leading schools?
- What is the precise role played by school leaders in fostering inclusive educational practices?
- How is social justice best fostered by school leaders?
- What specific educational leadership strategies reduce the black/white achievement gap?
- How might school leaders implement an effective data-driven, decision-making process in their schools?
- What are the critical factors affecting high performance among principals?
- What is the role of school leaders in reducing school violence?

- How do leadership practices positively influence school-community partnerships?
- What is the association between transformational leadership and teacher self-efficacy?
- How does shared leadership affect school morale and productivity?
- How do various types or forms of leadership impact organizational effectiveness?
- What are the social, cultural, political, and historical factors that influence the practice of educational leadership in different countries?
- How do leadership practices vary in differing contexts, social, cultural, or otherwise?
- What are the theoretical and practical differences among educational administration, management, and leadership?
- Why is an international perspective so critical for better understanding the challenges of leading schools in the twenty-first century?
- How can school leaders address race and identity, bias and privilege, and racialized current events?
- How can comparative research studies help us better understand educational leadership?
- What can we learn from studying educational leaders beyond the school level (e.g., district and Ministry [or Board] of Education leaders)?
- To what extent does emotional labor impact educational leaders?
- How can principals encourage action research and other alternatives to supervision to enhance teacher professional growth?
- How do school leaders effectively implement new technologies not just for the sake of technology but to deepen learning and provide better support for teachers?
- What are the consequences of workload on school leaders (e.g., the principal, or others) on their effectiveness as a leader?
- What are the challenges that school leaders face in differing regional contexts?
- How do school leaders develop the skills and knowledge they need to understand teachers' and students' needs and effectively guide learning?
- How do effective school leaders balance administrative duties with instructional priorities?
- What new educational management strategies can help teachers better confront classroom behavioral issues?
- How do school leaders coordinate curriculum and instructional initiatives across schools?
- Given time and budget constraints, how can school leaders find the resources to support an artful education (music, dance, creative writing, etc.) for all students?

- How do increased efforts to promote teacher leadership impact the work of principals and their assistants?
- What new innovative ideas can principals implement to deal with the increasingly complex landscape of curriculum today?
- How can principals support teacher-led professional development?
- What is the role of identity in fostering principal self-efficacy?
- How can school leaders help schools become more integral to their surrounding communities—and how can they better leverage community resources and connections to support their students and teachers?
- How can we better balance interest and work in instructional leadership with other important leadership responsibilities?
- How can districts support assistant principals and prepare new principals as they take the helm of the school?
- How do we induct and sustain good principals?
- How can we best prepare future school leaders?

Most fundamentally, the Rowman & Littlefield School Leadership Series is premised on the need to connect theory to practice. Each of these questions rely on a sound theoretical base that has important, if not critical relevance to the world of practice. This international series, in other words, reflects the latest cutting-edge theories and practices in school leadership that attempt to bridge the perennial divide between theory and practice.

Although we look to publish manuscripts that have relevance to an international audience, we will accept more localized research that might only be applicable in a specific context. The manuscript, of course, must meet the rigors of academic research and have significant impact on practice. Feel free to query the series editor to react to any ideas.

The series motto is framed after Kurt Lewin's famous statement, and we paraphrase, there is no sound theory without practice, and no good practice that is not framed on some theory. Authors are expected to illustrate the intimate and integral connection between the two divides. In this respect, we are unique because we do not accept proposals that are "heavy" on one side or the other; rather we look for manuscripts that are intellectually engaging, with a sound theoretical base, yet firmly grounded in the daily lives of school leaders.

I welcome readers to join the effort to increase knowledge in our field and affect daily school practice by submitting a proposal on any of the topics mentioned above, or any other relevant ones. Feel free to communicate with the series editor via email at yosglanz@gmail.com.

As series editor, I would like to take this opportunity to thank my latest advisory board, listed below, for their efforts in seeing the series to fruition. Their feedback to the authors and the editor was instrumental in crafting a well-researched, practical, and readable volume.

Köksal Banoğlu, Chief project executive at Maltepe District Governorship, Istanbul—Turkey
Clair T. Berube, Virginia Wesleyan University—Virginia Beach, VA—USA
Yin Cheong Cheng, The Education University of Hong Kong—Tai Po—Hong Kong
Mary Lynne Derrington, University of Tennessee, Knoxville, TN—USA
Sedat Gumus, Necmettin Erbakan University—Konya—Turkey
Sonya D. Hayes, University of Tennessee—Knoxville, TN—USA
Helen M. Hazi, West Virginia University at Morgantown, West Virginia—USA
Albert Jimenez, Kennesaw State University—Kennesaw, GA—USA
Benjamin Kutsyuruba, Queen's University—Kingston, ON—Canada
Orly Shapira-Lishchinsky, Bar Ilan University—Ramat Gan—Israel
Jane Wilkinson, Monash University—Victoria—Australia

Special acknowledgment is extended to Tom Koerner (vice president and publisher for education issues) and Kira Hall (assistant editor) for their support. I hope this volume and the series will receive wide acknowledgment for making a difference in the field of educational leadership.

As series editor, I am excited to introduce this latest volume of our series coedited by Dr. Alyson L. Lavigne and Dr. Mary Lynne Derrington, both with a wealth of experience in the field of educational leadership.

Alyson's research interests are broad, yet deep. Specializing in teacher education and instructional leadership, she has published on teacher retention, teachers' beliefs, teacher supervision and evaluation, and culturally and linguistically minoritized students' experiences. Yet, related to this work, she is well-versed on the research and practice of effective feedback, which is critical for improving teaching practices.

Mary Lynne is a former school superintendent, principal, and teacher. She is a scholar of instructional supervision having served as chair of the Supervision and Instructional Leadership AERA SIG. She also serves on our advisory board for the Rowman & Littlefield School Leadership Series.

A perusal of the contents page of *Actionable Feedback to PK–12 Teachers* is impressive. The wide array of scholars and practitioners who contributed chapters gives evidence to the importance of the relationship between supervision and feedback.

This volume fits beautifully within the theme and purpose of the Rowman & Littlefield School Leadership Series because it clearly bridges theory with practice. The first section of *Actionable Feedback to PK–12 Teachers* presents a comprehensive and varied review of extant research in supervision related specifically to feedback. The second half of the book helps readers to connect this research and theory to the real world of practice. Specifically, this section provides practical strategies of feedback in various academic disciplines, school contexts, and given the world's recent move to online learning, in virtual spaces.

Personally, I believe that working with teachers in the classroom to improve teaching practice through constructive and meaningful feedback is a prime focus of instructional supervision. Recently, I argued for more research and emphasis on supervision as experienced and practiced in the classroom (Glanz, 2022). Feedback in this context is critical to good supervision. This edited volume is very much welcomed, and I believe it will increase attention to this aspect of supervision, often ignored in the overall literature in the field of educational supervision.

I am without doubt that this work on supervision and feedback will find a receptive audience worldwide. Although there are a few other works on this topic, the editors have made a unique contribution above and beyond others. They have masterfully combined the vast research and work on the subject with practical and helpful suggestions for educators, scholars, and practitioners alike.

I believe *Actionable Feedback to PK–12 Teachers* will draw wide attention to this needed subject and will likely become the go-to book in the field. This work is an important contribution to our field, and on behalf of the advisory board, I thank the editors as well as the experienced and talented contributors for a work that will certainly make a difference by improving teaching and increasing learning in K–12 classrooms.

Jeffrey Glanz
July 8, 2022

REFERENCE

Glanz, J. (2022). Personal reflections on supervision as instructional leadership: From whence it came and to where shall it go? *Journal of Educational Supervision,* 4(3). https://doi.org/10.31045/jes.4.3.5

Editors' Introduction

A school leader has many responsibilities and none more important than leading teacher development through effective supervision. While the definitions of teacher supervision vary, one common feature they share is a focus on supporting teacher growth, development, and improvement. Under the umbrella of teacher supervision, a common strategy to improve teachers' instructional practice is observation and feedback. While teachers may be observed by various individuals, the authors of this text recognize that for principals, observation of and feedback to teachers is key to improving teaching and learning.

However, ineffective feedback following observation has negative consequences. While school leaders are often perceived by their teachers to be fair, trustworthy, and accurate, they struggle to provide rich feedback. Specifically, principals are reluctant to provide content-based feedback, which is relatively absent from postobservation conferences since principals often observe teachers outside of their own areas of expertise. As such, principals usually provide general suggestions—feedback that teachers often perceive as not useful.

Peer coaching and other forms of teacher-led observation and feedback are gaining traction internationally as a promising practice. However, in places like the United States, such practices are underutilized, and principals will hold primary responsibility for observing and providing teachers with feedback now and well into the future. Without a massive overhaul of traditional structures of teacher supervision to reduce principals' loads, it is unrealistic to expect principals to possess the same rich expertise as a peer coach.

This text helps those responsible for teacher supervision to gain knowledge on best feedback practices tailored to classroom specific content and programs. The authors in section I summarize existing foundational and theoretical work on supervision and key effective feedback characteristics that apply across content areas. Section II chapter authors address two critical dimensions of supervision—content and context—to help teacher supervisors provide specific feedback. Together the two sections provide the big picture of supervision and its application to content and program areas.

Guiding questions that introduce each chapter help teacher supervisors focus their reading. Following the guiding questions, the content of each chapter helps expand or establish relevant knowledge for feedback. The reflection activities at the end of each chapter help teacher supervisors integrate these understandings into their feedback practices.

Our goal is to offer concrete ways for school leaders to proactively incorporate specific feedback into their supervision practice for increased teacher development and to demonstrate strong instructional leadership skills. That includes offering high-quality feedback, providing suggestions that are specific (not general), and advancing equity in their instructional supervision tasks.

We were delighted by the chapters written by well-known and respected authors. We encourage readers to reflect on the book content in its entirety as well as on detailed reading of each chapter. Readers might also find content most applicable to their practice. We welcome your feedback as we collectively learn best practices in teacher supervision.

SECTION I

The Big Picture of Supervision and Feedback

CHAPTER 1

Promising Supervisory Theories and Strategies for Instructional Improvement

Helen M. Hazi

PREFOCUS GUIDING QUESTIONS

- What experiences have you had with feedback from your principal (or supervisor)? What made the feedback useful?
- When and how do teachers change their practice?
- What goals do you have to improve teachers' in-classroom teaching?

INTRODUCTION

Various theories have influenced supervision over time. In its earliest days, authors with a focus on teaching, and influenced by educational psychology, explained Edward L. Thorndike's principles of learning to teachers who had little formal education. These authors thought of themselves as expert teachers and teacher educators.

Authors with a focus on administration, influenced by Frederick Taylor's efficiency movement, pursued the most efficient observation instrument and concepts to promote effective schools and the educators in them. Over time, most moved away from writing about teaching and principles of learning to focus on the "more modern" notion of supervision as efficiency (Hazi, 2020).

By the late 1970s and 1980s in the "golden age of supervision," academics looked to theories of administration to understand supervision in schools. Sergiovanni and Starratt (1979), Alfonso, Firth, and Neville (1981), and Firth and Pajak (1998) used theories about organizations, leadership, communication, and decision making. In fact, change theory was used to explain how to improve teaching, and feedback emerged as the principal's primary tool.

Feedback is considered the transmission of evaluative or corrective information about a person's performance on a task. Principals were encouraged to deliver frequent, timely, consistent, specific, and private feedback. At the time, this advice was helpful and echoed advice about giving feedback to students in the learning process (Hattie, 2012).

Today advice about feedback abounds. In a recent issue of *Educational Leadership* advice is offered about feedback triggers, misconceptions, three ingredients of a feedback culture, and five characteristics of what feedback teachers want. Most advice seems helpful and based on experiences; however, information about teacher learning seems missing, yet important.

To this end, this chapter offers theories and promising strategies that support teacher learning. The chapter includes sections on the teacher change approach, the teacher learning approach, and a new mindset for what's missing from our thinking (i.e., evidence, relationships, and promising supervisory practices). The term *supervisor* is used to mean those department chairs, teacher leaders, mentors, coaches, and principals, when they work with teachers to help them improve their practice.

The Teacher Change Approach

The teacher change approach has dominated our thinking about teacher learning. It took root in the early days of schooling when teaching was a chance occupation for women and limited courses existed prior to their employment. In fact, supervisors with the same content specialization and principals were responsible to improve teachers. It was assumed that teachers were weak and classroom visitation was designed to find fault.

As teachers objected to such classroom inspection, they considered in-service training outside of classrooms more palatable. In-service training took many forms: book study, conventions, course attendance, curriculum work, demonstration teaching, faculty workshops, institutes, publishing articles, and exchange teaching (Spears, 1953). As preparation programs evolved from single courses, this view of teacher learning dominated practice and writings.

Classical behavioral theory, change theory, and process-product research came to influence this approach. Educators believed that teacher knowledge, made up of discrete and independent behaviors, became obsolete and needed updating.

Teacher evaluation was based on generic teaching behaviors identified by the process-product research. These common behaviors correlated with increases in student achievement regardless of lesson, subject, grade, or student ability. They include questioning, wait time, praise and criticism, giving directions, clarifying student ideas, and use of advance organizers. Teacher effectiveness was judged on the frequency of behavior (e.g., Brophy & Good, 1986). With regular observation, the principal delivered suggestions for improvement that the teacher was to change before the next visit.

It was also thought that knowledge came from consultants and research, external to teachers and delivered in "one-shot" workshops with tips and worksheets. In turn, workshops delivered specific and concrete bits of knowledge that could apply to most teaching situations. This view of learning influenced how educators thought about teachers and their improvement. Principals improved teacher knowledge by providing workshops and delivering feedback focused on these trainings.

However, some saw this view as flawed, as research showed that some teachers did not find evaluator feedback useful and innovations faded when workshop vendors no longer supported their products. Also, this view may have overestimated the role of principals in improvement for those who did not have the time, will, or expertise. This had become a *deficit view* of teacher skill and knowledge.

The Teacher Learning Approach

In the mid-1980s, cognitive psychologists helped move thinking from focusing on teacher behaviors alone to include their knowledge structures, and portrayed teacher learning as complex, unpredictable, and contextualized. Teachers were considered active agents of their learning and "reflective practitioners" (Schon, 1983).

Lee Shulman (1987) helped advance research on *pedagogical content knowledge*. Teacher educators and researchers began to study how specialized knowledge in science, mathematics, language arts, and social studies was needed for "choosing appropriate examples, selecting representations to highlight particular features of the content, anticipating student difficulties, and interpreting student insights" (Russ et al., 2016, p. 398).

Many hope that such pedagogy promotes *ambitious instruction* that has demanding learning goals so that "all students encounter subjects in ways that more closely resemble disciplinary and other real-world contexts" (Spillane & Jennings, 1997, p. 449). Furthermore, because this knowledge depends on context, feedback on generic teaching behaviors found on many current evaluation forms may be less useful to some. By extension then, supervisors may need to situate their feedback in a lesson's purpose, content, grade, and student ability levels to be helpful to teachers.

It is important to realize that there is no consensus on what effective teaching is, despite the many evaluation instruments and standards on which they are based. "Right now, the field is in the midst of trying to articulate what a set of core practices might look like" that both describe the practice and explain its purpose (Kennedy, 2016, p. 8).

As these understandings about teaching are evolving, how do supervisors talk about teaching? Supervisors can generate evidence to help teachers learn in the context of their classrooms and co-construct a vocabulary about that learning. It may be that, when teachers name what they do, they can come to understand and grow in their practice (Garman, 1986). A supervisor's goal then should be to promote teacher learning both in and outside of their classrooms through observations, conversations, and active engagement individually and collectively in groups.

A New Mindset About Teaching and Its Improvement

Supervisors need to think differently about teaching and its improvement. It may be time to consider that teachers are unique individuals, constructing various types of knowledge over time, and transforming knowledge into action for student learning. While supervisors are advised to have in-depth conversations with them, what are possible topics? Supervisors can help teachers think about and construct their own unique signature, knowledge maps, routines, and instructional purposes of the curriculum they hope to teach to students.

Teachers have their own unique *teaching signature* (Eisner, 1991) and map of knowledge about content, learning, and pedagogy. This signature evolves over a career as teachers grow in and learn from their practice. Constructivism, a theory of learning and mindset, helps explain how teachers acquire knowledge. Knowledge of teaching is highly personalized and best understood as actively constructed and reconstructed as teachers learn from their practice. This map includes some of their earliest experiences observing teaching from their childhood. By talking and reflecting, teachers can discover and develop their own signature.

"The knowledge teachers need to teach well and to improve themselves is embedded in the . . . actions they undertake" (Runhaar et al., 2010). Because teachers do a high volume of learning, they require a deep understanding of content and, at times, must *unlearn* some of what they once learned. In their knowledge structures, teachers may do the following: simply add new knowledge, substantially modify and restructure existing knowledge, or fine tune existing knowledge structures where minor changes can be made (Russ et al., 2016). These processes will likely depend on the teacher, what they know, and how they learn.

Some believe that teachers think in routines and change them when they no longer work with students. *Routines* are short plans that guide activity and contain common behaviors, such as "systems for determining how students will be called on, how materials will be distributed, and how assignments will be collected and returned" (Kennedy, 2005, p. 83). A routine develops when needed, then evolves as a teacher tinkers and shapes it.

Curriculum has a place in supervision. Before school begins, teachers are challenged first by dividing content into weekly and daily segments, then how to portray curriculum content so that naïve minds can construct and reconstruct their own mental maps of knowledge over time.

Lesson plans "represent their strategy for enacting the curriculum, for converting a passive textbook into live activities" (Kennedy, 2016, p. 10). A teacher uniquely plans lessons around activities that unfold over time based on their personal and professional judgments.

Teachers also need to know the *instructional purpose* that an action serves. "Clarity about purposes is especially important for novices because novices themselves hold many misconceptions about what teachers do and why" (Kennedy, 2016, p. 9). There is no one "correct way" to portray content, but many. Kennedy emphasizes that we should "evaluate a lesson according to how its content is portrayed" (2016, p. 11). Therefore, supervisors should ask, "Was the purpose(s) of the lesson accomplished?" This can be an important question because it is rarely asked. Evidence will be needed to help address it, and make its answer visible in the classroom.

Evidence

Most teacher evaluation instruments in use today are designed to rate teacher action and behavior—not collect evidence. Evidence has been missing from teacher evaluation and from most feedback. Yet evidence is what will help teachers take charge of their own learning, which they must, if improvement is to occur. This section will address why evidence is important in supervision and how evidence can help teachers study their practice.

Evidence is defined as information that helps teacher and supervisor study teaching. Evidence broadly includes records of what occurred in the classroom, student confusions and learnings in the lesson, and classroom artifacts (i.e., lesson plans, worksheets, pacing guides, and teacher-made tests).

Teacher and observer need a record of the lesson to better understand teacher thinking, student performance, teacher strengths, and/or goals for improvement, if, and when warranted. Cogan (1973) advocates for a record to replace selective noticing and poor recollections of what did and did not transpire. Such records guard against premature judgment or "judg[ing] rigidly or too rapidly" (p. 41).

Supervisor and teacher should jointly plan the observation so that evidence is situated in the lesson to be more useful. When the teacher joins in deciding on the focus and evidence, this helps minimize questions about the authenticity of the record, and "help[s] to strengthen the professional relationship between teacher and supervisor and expedite[s] their work together" (Cogan, 1973, p. 137). The challenge will be to make it meaningful and not trivial.

Evidence can come from an observation form as simple as a seating chart or room diagram, a checklist of best practices in a subject or of errors on homework, or audio or video recordings. Sometimes it may be a frequency count of behaviors of a single student, or a pattern in questioning of the class. Sullivan and Glanz (2013) offer many examples of forms.

To explore whether the goals of the lesson were accomplished, the supervisor and teacher could review the lesson plan, district standards, and curriculum guide (artifacts) in a preconference to decide on what evidence is needed. If students discuss in groups a series of teacher-posed questions, the observer could collect teacher directions for discussion (observer notes), which groups were on and off-task (room diagram), and content of the answers each group, either recorded (student artifacts) or reported (observer notes). Both teacher and supervisor can have evidence to evaluate whether each group accomplished the lesson's objectives.

When the teacher gives a quiz, each student's score would also provide evidence. The supervisor can offer some or all options for judging the success of a lesson or any of its segments.

If one must use the district form and give feedback, then the supervisor should review the lesson and curriculum plan, collect specific examples and where they appear in the lesson, and learn about the students. This helps the supervisor see the teacher in context of the lesson, students, and the curriculum, instead of simply fitting the teacher to a form. If content expertise is required, a second observer can provide needed insight and, if necessary, corroboration. Some of this information can be acquired in a conference prior to the observation or at the start of the postconference.

Relationships

In principle, teachers endorse supervision; but in reality, they severely limit it (Blumberg, 1974). This ambivalence reported in earlier decades is likely found in current times when teachers say they want to improve but report that principal feedback is not useful. Relationships are built one conversation at a time.

Supervisors often assume that they are in relationship with teachers who are open, willing, and receptive to what they have to offer. While the organization may grant supervisors legitimacy to enter classrooms, teachers may present a "façade of interest" or "pretend to listen." However, "[t]he teacher, not the supervisor, controls supervision. It is the teacher who permits or refuses access to self, and it is the supervisor who needs to obtain an invitation. . . ." (Blumberg & Jonas, 1987, p. 59). Teachers will "open the door" to individuals who give nonpunitive feedback.

Developing a relationship is hard work and can be easily broken. Teachers must trust and have confidence in their supervisors. It is not established with simple advice, such as "talk less, listen more"; use "we" and make a "sandwich"; or wrapping negative feedback between two positives. Teachers are less receptive to negative feedback and criticism (Ilgen et al., 1979), but can be receptive to feedback that they can control such as motivating and managing students.

Supervisors should become colleagues. Collegiality is "the particular frame of mind one brings to educational encounters" that are face-to-face between or among willing participants (Garman, 1982, p. 39). Garman (1986) wants the teacher and supervisor working together side-by-side, deciding on the observation focus, planning the lesson in a preconference, and reviewing evidence and discussing the lesson in the postconference. Both listen, are genuinely open, and co-construct knowledge in a collaborative approach where both learn.

Promising Strategies for Teacher Learning

Instructional improvement is a complex process difficult for one person to accomplish. Perhaps supervisors should think of improvement as a system with multiple strategies that promote teacher learning in different ways. Two decades of research suggest that some promising strategies have had a positive impact on teachers, and, in some cases, their students. They include mentoring, professional development, formative assessment, National Board Certification, coaching, professional learning communities, and teacher advice networks. Each strategy includes a brief description and an explanation of barriers or conditions for success.

Mentoring

When beginning teachers are provided mentors: their job satisfaction and retention increase; they focus on student on-task behavior, student questioning, classroom climate, and management; and they can increase student achievement. Programs vary in terms of length, mentor selection, training, and pay. The most influential factors are selection and training of same-subject mentors, common planning time, and regularly scheduled collaboration (Ingersoll & Strong, 2011).

Professional Development

Programs that engage teachers in classroom-based problem solving and help them "see" their own classrooms differently have "the greatest positive impact on teachers' effectiveness" (Kennedy, 2019, p. 157). In these programs, teachers are introduced to new research, plan lessons, and report the result of lessons taught. Hill (2020) found that when teachers used new curriculum on their colleagues, as if they were students, before using them in their own classrooms, they learn the mistakes students typically make with the materials.

Formative Assessment

Teachers use the results of student in-class work, teacher-made tests, and conversations with students and their parents to guide their next plans for instruction. Formative assessment is assessment *for* learning. Supervisors can build a culture that supports data use with goals and high expectations; opportunities for teacher collaboration; and resources of time, training and technology (Hoogland et al., 2016). Supervisors can help teachers: collect and analyze different types of evidence about student learning, identify problems and causes of poor performance, and make improvements based on the evidence.

National Board for Professional Teaching Standards

To promote teacher quality, the National Board for Professional Teaching Standards (NBPTS) was founded by teachers as a national, voluntary certification process in 1987. Teachers, judged by other board-certified teachers, take a content test, submit a portfolio of work samples, video record interactions with students, and reflect on their practice. Teachers apply what they learn in their classrooms, gain a new enthusiasm for teaching, and become mentors and coaches to other teachers. This year-long process has been an effective professional learning opportunity for over 40,000 U.S. teachers in 25 certificate areas (Lustick & Sykes, 2006).

Coaching

Coaching grew as a practice out of frustration, when summer workshops failed to result in improvement during the school year (Showers & Joyce, 1996). Coaches, especially in reading and math, improve instruction when they engage in one-to-one, intensive, subject-specific, and sustained work with teachers; and when combined with group training, demonstrations, instructional content material and video examples. Coaching is successful when there is teacher buy-in, a culture that supports constructive feedback, and released time (Kraft et al., 2018).

Professional Learning Communities

Professional learning communities (PLCs) are "teams of teachers committed to meeting on a regular basis to examine their teaching practices, the strategies they use, and the effects of those practices on the students with whom they work" (Arredondo Rucinski, 2016, p. 3). They tend to positively impact student learning in elementary and middle schools where teachers already work in teams, and where there is a culture of inquiry.

Teacher Advice Networks

Advice networks are informal ways that teachers seek advice from teachers in their own subject or grade level. These networks provide "high depth" coaching (e.g., analysis of student work that helps modify instruction) during teacher collaborative time in as well as outside of school. They are also successful when principal and coach attend professional development, have frequent meetings, and jointly visit classrooms (Garrison Wilhelm et al., 2018).

Some promising strategies may fit better into a school than others. One strategy may appeal to some teachers, more than others. The emphasis should be on choice and multiple options when promoting teacher learning.

CONCLUSION

A deficit view of teaching and its improvement dominated at a time when we knew little about how teachers learn. This view was largely influenced by change theory, classic behavioral theory, and a focus on generic teaching behaviors. While feedback on behavior has been considered the primary way to change teachers, we have learned its limitations. As research has evolved under the influence of cognitive psychology and pedagogical content knowledge, teachers are seen differently as unique in their knowledge and practice and in need of different avenues for improvement.

This chapter has identified what has been missing from our thinking about instructional improvement: a focus on teacher learning instead of delivering feedback, the importance of evidence and relationships, and multiple strategies for teacher learning. Promising strategies include mentoring, professional development, formative assessment, National Board Certification, coaching, professional learning communities, and teacher advice networks.

"As we have become more aware of the many contingencies involved in teaching, we have shifted our focus away from telling teachers what to do and toward deepening their understanding of their students so that they can make better in-the-moment judgments about how to respond to students" (Kennedy, 2019, p. 147). Teacher learning must be at the center of our thinking about their improvement.

POSTREADING REFLECTIONS/ACTIVITIES

- Using your current school as the context, develop a plan to improve teaching. What are your goals, system of promising strategies, and school routines?
- Observe a teacher's lesson. In one part, use a seating chart to collect evidence on teacher and/or student behavior(s) appropriate to the lesson. In another, use your district's observation form. What are the differences? Which was more useful for you and for the teacher, and why?
- With a lesson plan, identify evidence to be collected to evaluate whether its purposes were accomplished. What insights does this provide about observation and evidence?

REFERENCES

Alfonso, R., Firth, G., & Neville, R. (1981). *Instructional supervision: A behavior system* (2nd ed.). Allyn & Bacon.

Arredondo Rucinski, D. (2016). *Real world professional learning communities: Their use and effects*. Rowman & Littlefield.

Blumberg, A. (1974). *Supervisors and teachers: A private cold war*. McCutchan.

Blumberg, A., & Jonas, R. (1987). Permitting access: The teacher's control over supervision. *Educational Leadership, 44*(8), 58–62. https://eric.ed.gov/?id=EJ353887

Brophy, J., & Good, T. (1986). Teacher behavior and student achievement. In M. Wittrock (Ed.), *Handbook of research on teaching* (3rd ed.) (pp. 328–75). Macmillan.

Cogan, M. (1973). *Clinical supervision*. Houghton Mifflin Company.

Darling-Hammond, L., Chung Wei, R., Andree, A., Richardson, N., & Orphanos, S. (2009, February). Professional learning in the learning profession: A status report on teacher development in the United States and abroad. National Staff Development Council and The School Redesign Network. https://edpolicy.stanford.edu/sites/default/files/publications/professional-learning-learning-profession-status-report-teacher-development-us-and-abroad.pdf

Eisner, E. (1991). *The enlightened eye: Qualitative inquiry and the enhancement of educational practice*. Macmillan.

Firth, G., & Pajak, E. (1998). *Handbook on school supervision*. Simon & Schuster Macmillan.

Garman, N. B. (1982). The clinical approach to supervision. In T. J. Sergiovanni (Ed.), *Supervision of teaching: The 1982 ASCD Yearbook* (pp. 35–52). Association for Supervision and Curriculum Development.

Garman, N. B. (1986). Clinical supervision: Quackery or remedy for professional practice. *Journal of Curriculum and Supervision, 1*(2), 148–57.

Garrison Wilhelm, A., Cobb, P., Frank, K., & I-Chen, C. (2018). Teachers' advice networks. In P. Cobb, K. Jackson, E. Henrick, T. Smith, & the MIST Team (Eds.), *Systems for instructional improvement: Creating coherence from the classroom to the district office* (pp. 135–48). Harvard Education Press.

Hattie, J. (2012). Feedback in schools. In R. Sutton, M. Hornsey, & K. Douglas (Eds.), *Feedback: The communication of praise, criticism, and advice* (pp. 265–77). Peter Lang.

Hazi, H. M. (2020). Instructional improvement: A modest essay. *Journal of Educational Supervision, 3*(3), 90–103. https://doi.org/10.31045/jes.3.3.7

Hill, H. (2020, February 21). Teacher PD gets a bad rap. But two approaches do work. *Education Week.* https://www.edweek.org/leadership/opinion-teacher-pd-gets-a-bad-rap-but-two-approaches-do-work/2020/02

Hoogland, I., Schildkamp, K., van der Kleij, F., Heitink, M., Kippers, W., Veldkamp, B., & Dijkstra, A. (2016). Prerequisites for data-based decision making in the classroom: Research evidence and practical illustrations. *Teaching and Teacher Education 60*, 377–86. https://doi.org/10.1016/j.tate.2016.07.012

Ilgen, D., Fisher, C., & Taylor, M. S. (1979). Consequences of individual feedback on behaviors in organizations. *Journal of Applied Psychology, 64*(4), 349–71. https://doi.org/10.1037/0021-9010.64.4.349

Ingersoll, R., & Strong, M. (2011). The impact of induction and mentoring programs for beginning teachers: A critical review of the research. *Review of Educational Research, 81*(2), 201–33. https://repository.upenn.edu/cgi/viewcontent.cgi?article=1127&context=gse_pubs

Kennedy, M. (2005). *Inside teaching.* Harvard University Press.

Kennedy, M. (2016). Parsing the practice of teaching. *Journal of Teacher Education, 67*(1), 6–17. https://doi.org/10.1177/0022487115614617

Kennedy, M. (2019). How we learn about teacher learning. *Review of Research in Education, 43*, 138–62. https://doi.org/10.3102/0091732X19838970

Kraft, M., Blazar, D., & Hogan, D. (2018). The effect of teaching coaching on instruction and achievement: A meta-analysis of the causal evidence. *Review of Educational Research, 88*(4), 547–88. https://scholar.harvard.edu/mkraft/publications/effect-teacher-coaching-instruction-and-achievement-meta-analysis-causal

Lustick, D., & Sykes, G. (2006). National board certification as professional development: What are teachers learning? *Education Policy Analysis Archives, 14*(5), 1–44. http://epaa.asu.edu/epaa/v14n5/

Runhaar, P., Sanders, K., Yang, H. (2010). Stimulating teachers' reflection and feedback asking: An interplay learning goal orientation, and transformational leadership. *Teaching and Teacher Education, 26*(5), 1154–1161. https://doi.org/10.1016/j.tate.2010.02.011

Russ, R. S., Sherin, B. L., & Gamoran Sherin, M. (2016). What constitutes teacher learning? In D. Gitomer & C. Bell's *Handbook of research on teaching 5th ed.* (pp. 391–438). American Educational Research Association.

Schön, D. (1983). *The reflective practitioner: How professionals think in action.* Basic.

Sergiovanni, T., & Starratt, J. (1979). *Supervision: Human perspectives* (2nd ed.). McGraw Hill.

Showers, B., & Joyce, B. (1996). The evolution of peer coaching. *Educational Leadership, 53*(6), 12–16. https://www.ascd.org/el/articles/the-evolution-of-peer-coaching

Shulman, L. S. (1987). Knowledge and teaching: Foundations of the new reform. *Harvard Educational Review, 57*(1), 1–22. http://hepg.org/her-home/issues/harvard-educational-review-volume-57,-issue-1/herarticle/foundations-of-the-new-reform_461

Spears, H. (1953). *Improving the supervision of instruction*. Prentice-Hall.
Spillane, J., & Jennings, N. (1997). Aligned instructional policy and ambitious pedagogy: Exploring instructional reform from the classroom perspective. *Teachers College Record, 98*(3), 449–81. https://doi.org/10.1177/016146819709800303
Sullivan, S., & Glanz, J. (2013). *Supervision that improves teaching and learning* (4th ed.). Corwin.

CHAPTER 2

Providing Feedback for Evaluation and Professional Learning

Monica Anthony, Wyatt Hall, Michael W. Krell, and Colleen Moore Eccles

PREFOCUS GUIDING QUESTIONS

- As a supervisor, how do you measure whether your feedback is successful?
- Have you noticed any relationships between your attitudes or dispositions and how teachers apply the feedback you give?
- How can feedback cultivate a trusting relationship between observers and teachers?

INTRODUCTION

This chapter focuses on theoretical understandings of feedback, what makes feedback effective, and how feedback, in its various forms, can support teacher growth and retention. Following a holistic perspective on feedback on teaching, this chapter addresses different types of feedback and delivery: evaluative, nonevaluative, immediate, and delayed. The guidance presented in this chapter is informed by seminal research on feedback and formative assessment, recent research on teacher professional learning, and the authors' collective expertise as a district-level mentor and university field supervisors.

THEORY OF FEEDBACK AND FORMATIVE ASSESSMENT

Feedback on teaching is crucial to improving teacher reflection, teacher practice, and ultimately student learning. Generally, effective feedback establishes where the learner is, identifies where the learner needs to be, and clarifies how to get from where they are to where they need to be (Black & Wiliam, 2009). Thus, effective feedback is instructional because it not only evaluates or corrects but identifies how to improve or how to meet a goal (Hattie & Timperley, 2007). Not only is the content of feedback important, but the timeliness and frequency of feedback also plays a role in its effectiveness.

Although feedback is typically provided by an observer to a teacher, the process is ultimately collaborative. Teachers should be invited to reflect on their practice, self-identify areas where feedback would be appreciated or beneficial, discuss the provided feedback to ensure comprehension and application, and then have opportunities to apply the feedback.

Engaging in this collaborative process enables mutual inquiry around the teacher's practice. Mutual inquiry is an aspect of self-directed learning, one of the key elements of adult learning theory (andragogy; Knowles et al., 2005). Adult learning theory also suggests when adult learners (in this case, teachers) are able to self-direct their learning, they are more motivated to apply the knowledge and feedback of others.

Feedback is only effective to the extent that it is applied by the receiver. Thus, any feedback from an observer must be provided in ways that are responsive to the disposition of the teacher. Teachers are not a cultural monolith. Teachers reflect the cultural variety of the world, and with these cultures comes written, verbal, and nonverbal norms around communication.

Communication styles embody cultural values and ways of knowing that influence how one engages with learning tasks, such as improving one's teaching practice (Gay, 2010). School leaders must consider cultural norms during the feedback process in order to best support their individual teachers.

School leaders would benefit from an awareness and appreciation for teachers' communication preferences when scheduling time for feedback, giving feedback, or planning next steps with a teacher. For example, what format should an observer use when sharing feedback: a rubric, an email, a verbal discussion? If a school leader shares ideas for next steps, should it be done in an email where references could be included, or in-person where the application can be discussed? Talking about preferred communication style can help school leaders deliver feedback in a way that is most accessible to the teacher.

CONNECTING FEEDBACK TO TEACHER RETENTION/ATTRITION

The principles and practices of providing feedback in this chapter aim to build trust and respect between school leaders and teachers in an effort to fight teacher attrition. Meaningful feedback is an important factor in supporting teachers and nurturing their self-efficacy and sense of autonomy.

Without constructive feedback and encouragement, the inevitable failures and setbacks novice teachers experience can become overwhelming, leading to feelings of inadequacy, lack of confidence, and an inability to persist in teaching (Grant, 2006).

The effects of teacher attrition on students, schools, and communities are well documented and wide reaching. The most recent national-level statistics, collected from 2011 to 2013, indicate that only about 18 percent of turnover is due to retirement, while around 67 percent is voluntary (Carver-Thomas & Darling-Hammond, 2019). With the majority of turnover being voluntary, educational leaders must look to what impacts teachers' decisions to leave the profession.

Although many factors that contribute to teacher attrition are outside the control of local school leaders (e.g., salary), there are school-level factors affecting teacher attrition over which leadership can exert some control. Research suggests that the degree to which teachers feel supported by administration impacts teacher attrition (Guarino et al., 2006; Ingersoll, 2001). This support is especially crucial in the first years of teaching, when turnover rates tend to be higher (Guarino et al., 2006). Furthermore, the stresses placed upon educators during the global COVID-19 pandemic are likely to increase attrition rates (Steiner & Woo, 2021).

Given this link between administrative support and early career attrition, the focus should be on "sustaining" teachers rather than "retaining" them (Schaefer et al., 2012). Teachers who feel supported in their practice and in their learning are more likely to stay in the profession (Buchanan et al., 2013; Johnson, 2012). Supporting teachers includes developing their sense of autonomy as well as their self-efficacy, both of which are linked to retention (Guarino et al., 2006). Grant (2006) defines self-efficacy as "the extent to which someone believes that [they] can successfully complete an action to produce a desired outcome" (p. 51).

Thus, while feedback on teaching is a key component in sustaining teachers to persist in the profession, it cannot perform this role alone (Grant, 2006). In fact, feedback can backfire and damage self-efficacy if not accompanied by appropriate support of other types. For example, if an administrator encourages a novice teacher to handle a specific classroom management issue—a major source of teacher burnout (Schaefer et al., 2012)—but then fails to provide any resources, modeling, or other visible support to the teacher to do so, this will discredit the administrator and further undermine the teacher's self-efficacy when they are unsuccessful.

HOW TO PROVIDE EVALUATIVE AND NONEVALUATIVE FEEDBACK

Given that feedback is crucial not only for improving teacher practice but improving teacher retention, how do school leaders evaluate teachers while at the same time provide them with feedback that promotes agency in their learning and the trusted space to grow? Research and practice show that both evaluative and nonevaluative feedback are required to develop and sustain educators. The rest of this chapter explores how to put the theories of effective feedback into action, illustrated with examples from teacher preparation, professional learning, and school-based coaching.

Evaluative Feedback

Evaluative feedback is a natural byproduct of formal observations and current teacher evaluation models (e.g., Framework for Teaching; Danielson, 2013). Observers and evaluators can work to foster trust and respect with teachers by grounding their feedback in observational data and the evaluation tools. Evaluative feedback can serve a formative role when it goes beyond rubric ratings and scores to include qualitative elements in the form of examples, suggestions, or next steps.

According to theories of andragogy, familiarity with performance assessments and evaluation criteria supports learners' desire to improve performance by enabling them to see for themselves the gaps between where they are and where they want to be (Knowles et al., 2005). Grounding observational feedback in the language of the evaluation criteria allows teachers to connect their feedback directly to the assessment. However, in order for performance assessments to be a learning tool, school leaders should ensure that teachers understand how to read and interpret the rubric ratings and criteria prior to any observations.

The following sections discuss the benefits of immediate and delayed feedback following observations. Regardless of when feedback is discussed with the observed teacher, written evaluations should not be finalized until afterward. Given the importance of reflection on practice, teachers should have opportunities to share the reasoning behind their in-the-moment decision making and to interpret any observational data before the observer shares their feedback. Furthermore, teachers know their students and their classrooms best and, thus, may provide the observer with additional context that better informs the observers' evaluation.

Immediate Observation Debrief and Feedback

Research indicates that feedback to teachers is more effective when provided as soon as possible after an observation (e.g., Brinko, 1993; Thurlings et al., 2013). In the authors' work with preservice teachers (PSTs) in secondary mathematics, they have found that debriefing immediately following an observation both positions PSTs as knowledgeable and capable of solving problems while also reflecting on the experience while it is in recent memory. In addition, immediate debriefs are valuable for troubleshooting and making adjustments before teaching the same lesson again to a new group of students.

The immediate postobservation debrief is centered on data collected by the observer. While teachers themselves might suggest a data collection focus, some examples of data to collect are questions asked by the teacher versus by students, tallies of which students participated and how, or types of formative assessments used.

The teacher is then provided time to reflect on the data and share what the data reveals to them about their practice. For example, student participation data may show that only a few students are volunteering to participate or that the teacher tends to call on students who sit in one section of the room. This reflection step is even more significant when the teacher decides what types of data they want the observer to collect.

Observer feedback is offered only after the teacher has reflected on the lesson and offered their own ideas regarding trends or realizations from the data. The feedback should connect the collected data to the performance assessment. Connecting the data to the language of the performance assessment allows the observer to clarify the teacher's current performance and what may be needed to reach the desired performance criteria. Then the teacher and observer would collectively develop goals and action steps to enable the teacher to improve their practice.

For example, when connecting to the Framework for Teaching (Danielson, 2013), student participation data shows few students actively engaged in the lesson, allowing many students to passively experience the lesson would be rated as "basic" under the element of Engaging Students in Learning. Hence, the observer and teacher would collaboratively determine how the teacher can provide more opportunities for students to show their thinking, such as the use of more open-ended tasks.

One of the benefits of immediately debriefing with data after a lesson is that the teacher can then apply their reflection and the received feedback to the next class session. In the event that the teacher teaches the same lesson again that day or the next, the observer can follow up about what changes were made. Asking, "What changes did you make and why did you make them?" invites the teacher to reflect on their decision making while also honoring their agency as professionals who are equipped to make instructional decisions that will benefit their students.

Finally, even though there was a verbal debrief, the observer should follow up with written feedback. This feedback would include both the data collected during the observation as well as suggestions and next steps based on the debrief conversation. Providing detailed written feedback after the observation and postobservation debrief have taken place allows for more specificity and better targeting of the feedback to the teacher's needs. In addition, teachers can return to and reference the written feedback when lesson planning or preparing for formal observations.

Delayed Observation Debrief and Feedback

While immediate feedback is widely supported in both fieldwork and research, there are distinct benefits for teachers when evaluators provide delayed feedback. In this model, teachers reflect on their lesson or practice prior to feedback being given by an evaluator or coach. This reframes the reflection process as happening prior to and during a feedback discussion, not simply after feedback has been given. Self-assessment and reflection are major components of formative assessment for our students, and should be integrated into the assessment of teachers as well.

Indeed, based on the authors' collective experience, when preservice and early career teachers have the opportunity to reflect, they do so deeply and in ways that grow their practice.

Although their focus may not be on what supervisors and school leaders may anticipate or see within the lesson, even novice teachers can introduce information crucial for unpacking the lesson.

For several years, one of the authors was a university supervisor to English-for-speakers- of-other-languages (ESOL) PSTs as they were completing their practicum experiences. After observations, PSTs were required to write up their reflection on the lesson and submit this reflection to him prior to the debrief together about the observed lesson.

PSTs' insights into their own practice were valuable, and they routinely shared mitigating factors he did not have immediate access to such as student formative assessment data, students' personal lives, and curricular demands unique to the content area, all which caused him to reshape his feedback and further his trust in the PSTs' abilities to recognize their areas for growth.

PSTs sharing their reflections ahead of time transforms the debrief from transmitting feedback on surface features of the lesson to a conversation about the teacher's deeper pedagogical thinking that may be only hinted at by the actions during the lesson. Reading the teacher's reflection and debriefing directly with the teacher before compiling his feedback allowed the supervisor to incorporate teacher input into his evaluation write-up. It also allowed teachers to shape their own next steps in ways they found realistic and applicable, which made these goals more likely to be integrated and acted upon in the next observation.

By first allowing the teacher to reflect on their own practice and set their own goals, teacher and supervisor can work together towards accurate evaluation and next steps, rather than reinforcing a power dynamic that denies teachers control over their own learning. In addition, when teachers are given the opportunity to set multiple goals, they very often incorporate their supervisor's feedback into at least one of those goals, if not many of the goals.

Based on data from his dissertation research involving PSTs (Hall, 2022), one of the authors found that at the end of every postobservation conference after everyone had shared their thoughts, PSTs created goals for themselves based on at least one of his documented areas of growth, despite having the latitude to set whatever goals they saw fit. When given the opportunity to set goals for herself after receiving feedback, one of the PSTs, Dez, chose as one of her goals to "reduce time dedicated to verbal directions while increasing the amount and quality of written/visual directions" (Hall, 2022, p. 165).

Furthermore, after the next observation, Dez rephrased the same goal and kept it as one of her ongoing goals: "Continue to match or mirror oral and written directions for a variety of activities." Setting goals is part of formative assessment, and having novice teachers set their own goals, allows them to own their growth process and incorporate evaluator feedback in a way that meets their teaching context.

Nonevaluative Feedback

While evaluative feedback can be an integral part of formative teacher assessment, nonevaluative feedback can be as well, and is often not as constrained in structure or implementation. Nonevaluative feedback is instructional notes, suggestions, or coaching that contributes to the teacher's professional growth without contributing to their evaluation. This feedback can be provided by a stakeholder who holds a nonevaluative role (e.g., a mentor teacher, instructional coach, peer observer) or provided by a stakeholder in an evaluative role but delivered in an informal structure (e.g., a classroom walkthrough).

Nonevaluative feedback serves as a way to contribute to teacher growth before, in between, or after formal observations. An instructional leader should also lay some of the groundwork for nonevaluative feedback processes, particularly to establish that nonevaluative feedback should happen routinely, be explicit in nature, and focus on teacher growth as the highest priority (Troen & Boles, 2014). The next section describes what some of these feedback structures can look like.

Different Formats for Nonevaluative Feedback

There are a variety of ways to provide nonevaluative feedback to teachers through observation. One way is instructional coaching from more experienced, job-alike teachers or from district personnel. Rather than reciprocal observations, the coach or mentor observes the teacher and provides feedback based on the teacher's goals. Instructional coaches are not evaluators; rather, they are collaborators who offer instructional, institutional, and emotional support to help foster teachers' professional visions (Lipton & Wellman, 2018).

Other forms of nonevaluative feedback can include walkthroughs, instructional rounds, and teacher rounds. Walkthroughs or learning walks can involve teachers with various amounts of experience being both observed or participating in a group that observes other teachers throughout the building. Walkthroughs are brief, usually for ten to fifteen minutes per classroom, visiting multiple classrooms.

Instructional rounds are quite similar to walkthroughs in length of time and visiting multiple classrooms but involve a different "host" teacher each time. They also involve a problem or question of practice to guide both observations and subsequent debriefs.

Teacher rounds involves a group of teachers and a host teacher picking a problem of practice each round, but rather than observing other teachers for 10 to 15 minutes each, the host teacher teaches a regular lesson and the rest of the group comes in to observe the entire lesson and debrief afterward, which forms the bulk of the round. While each of these forms of professional learning can provide feedback to teachers, they do not do so equally or toward the same purpose.

Challenges and Benefits of Nonevaluative Feedback

These forms of nonevaluative feedback can vary in their purpose and participant involvement, and the benefits of these forms of professional learning can also vary. Coaching can provide teachers with feedback on areas of growth that the observee chooses, giving them agency in their professional learning and increasing their investment in the process through individually tailored feedback. However, while teachers may get individually tailored feedback from their coach, they may be isolated from what other teachers, either novice or experienced, are doing in their classrooms.

Walkthroughs provide teachers with feedback from a number of individuals. Novice teacher participation in the observation process of walkthroughs can also expose them to a variety of forms of classroom instruction, which can provide them with indirect feedback on their own instruction. Instructional rounds provide similar benefits, and both can help cultivate a community of practice that supports teacher growth when enacted routinely.

However, the authors have found that feedback from walkthroughs and instructional rounds does not often reach the observed teachers, and even participation in walkthrough groups may not be enough structure in terms of what to observe for novice teachers to make the most of the opportunity. Furthermore, the briefness of observations during walk-throughs and instructional rounds can make it difficult to get a deep sense of teacher decision making.

Teacher rounds respond to some of these challenges by focusing on only one lesson for the observation and allowing the observed teacher to set a problem of practice as a focal point for the observation. While opening up one's classroom to others for observations by peers can be a daunting task, having a mixed-experience group of novice and more experienced teachers allows for the more experienced teachers to go first, which models vulnerability, respect, and trust for more reticent teachers. Since all teachers in the group will have the opportunity to host at least once, every teacher inhabits the role of host and observer.

Keeping the rounds group smaller and maintaining norms such as "no hogs, no logs" (no one dominates the conversation, and no one is a passive observer) can ensure that every teacher regardless of experience has a voice within the group. This is crucial for novice teachers, who often feel that they do not have as much of a right to give feedback to others. Teacher rounds can flatten the hierarchy of status within the group, especially when limited to sizes of four or five, as each participant inhabits all roles and the groups are too small for individuals to participate passively.

Beyond flattening the hierarchy and honoring teacher agency, teacher rounds are designed to avoid explicit evaluation of peers. The protocols and guiding questions introduced by Troen and Boles (2014) keep the focus on what has been collectively seen and heard during the observation regarding the problem of practice (not just analysis), and on next steps.

In one of the authors' dissertation research (Hall, 2022), one of the mentor teachers claimed that rounds had a kind of "nonthreateningness" to it, even in comparison to other forms of professional learning. This teacher compared this to her other observations, saying, "There's pressure when you do formal observations, or when you write a lesson plan, to stick to the lesson plan. The rounds allow you to be more flexible with what teachers are going to look for" (Hall, 2022, p. 158). This flexibility and the protocol's adherence to what is collectively seen and heard gives all teachers the opportunity to teach in a space of respect, trust, and vulnerability.

Teacher rounds can benefit both the novice teachers and their mentors. In his dissertation research, one of the authors found that how the PSTs framed and interpreted the collective teaching practice of the group influenced how one of the mentor teachers taught afterward. After observing both PSTs, the mentor reported that they were "more aware of the problems of practice that we were all bringing up in rounds . . . more intentional with lessons moving forward. I added more scaffolding to lessons. I took the time to more slowly build up to independent work by adding more 'we do' examples in my lessons" (Hall, 2022, p. 182).

While this quote represents the bridging of a larger disparity between experience levels, it also represents a further empowerment of teachers to shape collective instructional practice and further their investment in their schools.

CONCLUSION

This chapter detailed ways to provide feedback to teachers that supports their learning and professional growth, while respecting their agency. Whether providing evaluative or nonevaluative feedback, observers and school leaders should view feedback as a collaborative process with teachers. Feedback on teaching should not only inform teachers of their current performance but provide them with suggestions, resources, and support to improve their practice. In addition, regardless of feedback structure, teachers need opportunities to reflect on their practice and be empowered to set goals for themselves.

POSTREADING REFLECTIONS/ACTIVITIES

- This chapter discussed qualities of effective feedback and how to deliver feedback to teachers in ways that respects their agency. What can evaluative feedback offer to teachers in your school that nonevaluative feedback cannot, and vice versa?
- What are your goals as an observer or an evaluator when you go in to observe? Do your goals align with the feedback you provide and the school climate you are trying to cultivate?
- How do you use delayed versus immediate feedback in your observations?
- What opportunities for teacher reflection are currently integrated into your observational process? How might those opportunities be expanded?

REFERENCES

Black, P., & Wiliam, D. (2009). Developing the theory of formative assessment. *Educational Assessment, Evaluation, and Accountability, 21*, 5–31.

Brinko, K. T. (1993). The practice of giving feedback to improve teaching. *The Journal of Higher Education, 64*(5), 574–93. https://doi.org/10.1080/00221546.1993.11778449

Buchanan, J., Prescott, A., Schuck, S., Aubusson, P., Burke, P., & Louviere, J. (2013). Teacher retention and attrition: Views of early career teachers. *Australian Journal of Teacher Education, 38*(3), 112–29. https://doi.org/10.14221/ajte.2013v38n3.9

Carver-Thomas, D., & Darling-Hammond, L. (2019). The trouble with teacher turnover: How teacher attrition affects students and schools. *Education Policy Analysis Archives, 27*(36), 1–32. https://doi.org/10.14507/epaa.27.3699

Danielson, C. (2013). *The framework for teaching: Evaluation instrument*. The Danielson Group.

Gay, G. (2010). *Culturally responsive teaching: Theory, research, and practice* (2nd ed.). Teachers College Press.

Guarino, C. M., Santibañez, L., & Daley, G. A. (2006). Teacher recruitment and retention: A review of the recent empirical literature. *Review of Educational Research, 76*(2), 173–208. https://doi.org/10.3102/00346543076002173

Grant, L. W. (2006). Persistence and self-efficacy: A key to understanding teacher turnover. *Delta Kappa Gamma Bulletin, 72*(2), 50–54.

Gudwin, D. M., & Salazar-Wallace, M. D. (2010). *Mentoring and coaching: A lifeline for teachers in a multicultural setting*. SAGE. https://dx.doi.org/10.4135/9781483350431

Hall, W. (2022). *Leveling the playing field: Rounds in pre-service ESOL teacher education*. [Doctoral dissertation, University of Maryland, College Park].

Hattie, J., & Timperley, H. (2007). The power of feedback. *Review of Educational Research, 77*(1), 81–112.

Ingersoll, R. M. (2001). Teacher turnover and teacher shortages: An organizational analysis. *American Educational Research Journal, 38*(3), 499–534. https://doi.org/10.3102/00028312038003499

Johnson, S. M. (2012). Having it both ways: Building the capacity of individual teachers and their schools. *Harvard Educational Review, 82*(1), 107–22. https://doi.org/10.17763/haer.82.1.c8515831m501x825

Knowles, M. S., Holton, E. F., & Swanson, R. A. (2005). *The adult learner: The definitive classic in adult education and human resource development*. Elsevier.

Lipton, L., & Wellman, B. (2018). *Mentoring matters: A practical guide to learning-focused relationships* (3rd ed.). MiraVia.

Mangan, M. (1995). *Building cross-cultural competence: A handbook for teachers*. Springfield: Illinois State Board of Education, Educational Equity Services. (ERIC Document Reproduction Service No. ED420166)

Schaefer, L., Long, J. S., & Clandinin, D. J. (2012). Questioning the research on early career teacher attrition and retention. *Alberta Journal of Educational Research, 58*(1), 106–21.

Steiner, E. D., & Woo, A. (2021). *Job-related stress threatens the teacher supply: Key findings from the 2021 State of the U.S. Teacher survey*. RAND Corporation. https://www.rand.org/pubs/research_reports/RRA1108-1.html

Thurlings, M., Vermeulen, M., Bastiaens, T., & Stijnen, S. (2013). Understanding feedback: A learning theory perspective. *Educational Research Review 9*(1), 1–15. https://doi.org/10.1016/j.edurev.2012.11.004

Troen, V., & Boles, K. (2014). *The power of teacher rounds: A guide for facilitators, principals, & department chairs*. Corwin.

CHAPTER 3

Developmental and Differentiated Feedback for Educators

Ellie Drago-Severson and Jessica Blum-DeStefano

> Feedback is everywhere. It's in what we say, what we don't say. What we do, how we do it. It's all around us.—Experienced principal, NYCDOE

PREFOCUS GUIDING QUESTIONS

- What comes to mind when you think about the word *feedback*?
- What is feedback?
- What is something you would like to get better at in terms of giving feedback?

INTRODUCTION

Feedback is one key lever for building the kind of internal capacity needed in today's world. In fact, offering feedback—so that others can hear it—is one of the *most* important ways educators—whether one is a supervisor, school leader, instructional coach, teacher leader—can transform instruction, leadership, schools, organizations, and systems—and grow. Yet, when and where do educators learn *how* to give feedback? How can they give and differentiate feedback so that others can really hear it, take it in, and act on it? And how might a developmental lens complement and augment current understandings of best practices for feedback?

To address these questions, this chapter explores how a developmental approach to feedback can help educators individually and collectively and across content areas build adults' capacity for leadership, coaching, supervision, instruction, and advanced professional learning to meet the adaptive challenges that define education and leadership today. Specifically, this chapter invites you to do the following:

- Explore common challenges and best practices about feedback generated from the wider literature (in both business and education);
- Learn about and/or deepen your understanding of constructive-developmental theory as a lens for further exploring and practicing a developmental approach to feedback;
- Understand, specifically, how tuning into four qualitatively different ways of knowing in adulthood through differentiated feedback can enable educators to better honor and care for the different ways of knowing adults bring to their work, leadership, collaboration, teams, professional learning communities (PLCs), and lives (i.e., how adults make sense of and interpret feedback experiences in qualitatively different ways);
- Explore practical strategies for enacting a developmental approach to feedback that others can best hear, take in, learn from, and act upon; and
- Engage in developmental action planning to apply key ideas to advance practice through actionable feedback.

We hope that this chapter helps with reimagining pathways to growth and to grow capacities in self and others. Please take a moment to reflect through free writing or free thinking about the following:

1. How often do you receive and give feedback to colleagues?
2. What is your greatest challenge in terms of giving and/or receiving feedback?
3. What is your biggest hope in reading this chapter?

SETTING THE STAGE:
COMMON FEEDBACK CHALLENGES AND STRATEGIES

While giving and receiving feedback have always been important in education and the business sector, in recent years there has been an increasing emphasis on feedback as a tool for school improvement. For example, feedback is a through-line in teacher and principal evaluations, coaching, mentoring, professional learning communities (PLCs), peer observation cycles, and popular feedback frameworks in school (Boudett et al., 2005; Danielson, 2011; Marshall, 2013). There also seems to be a general consensus that "good" feedback is clear, consistent, relevant, and actionable (Marshall, 2013; Stone & Heen, 2015).

Despite this strong emphasis on feedback's potentiality and the growing body of core knowledge about best practices, principals, district-level leaders, and teachers often share that feedback is one of the "hardest" parts of their work. Educators name common challenges like not getting enough feedback, getting too much, getting only superficial or overly "nice" feedback, getting conflicting feedback from different sources, or getting feedback that just doesn't line up with their professional needs and goals (Danielson, 2011; Drago-Severson & Blum-DeStefano, 2016, 2018; Harris et al., 2014; Lavigne & Good, 2013; MacDonald, 2011; Marshall, 2013).

There is also a strong sense from feedback givers that, despite great investments of time and care, formal feedback systems do not fully yield the benefits they seek (Hallinger et al., 2014) and can often feel too constraining or one-size-fits all. This is where a developmental lens is key! While these feedback challenges undoubtedly have multiple roots and causes, an understanding of adult development helps illuminate *why* feedback can feel like such a moving target, and also *how* to scaffold feedback that really supports individual and organizational improvement. This chapter sheds light on the potential of employing a developmental lens.

THE PROMISE OF A DEVELOPMENTAL LENS: FEEDBACK FOR GROWTH

When thinking about feedback that is aimed truly at growth and capacity building—rather than, say, compliance—looking through a developmental lens can bring clarity both to what's been going well with feedback in education and also what's been missing. Infusing developmental attunement and sensitivity into feedback practices can help leaders and teachers offer feedback so others can better "hear"—and build a more collaborative, compassionate, inclusive culture of feedback giving and receiving. With this in mind, we turn next to key tenets of development in adulthood.

Adult developmental theory—and constructive-developmental theory in particular (Drago-Severson, 2004, 2009, 2012; Drago-Severson & Blum-DeStefano, 2016, 2018; Kegan, 1982, 1994)—posits three key ideas that inform a developmental approach to feedback. Specifically, the theory underscores that

- Adults make sense of and interpret the world in different ways. According to research, adults *take in* and make sense of the world with qualitatively different meaning making systems, or *ways of knowing*. These ways of knowing inform how educators both give and receive feedback, so understanding them can help create a roadmap for differentiating feedback supports and challenges.
- Adults can continue to grow—*on the inside*—throughout life, but only with appropriate supports and challenges. Constructive-developmental

theory also posits that growth can continue throughout the lifespan—along cognitive, affective, interpersonal, and intrapersonal lines—but requires just-right conditions. Toward these ends, collaboration, feedback, and developmental stretches that meet adults where they are can help scaffold growth and transformation.
- Adults need *different* kinds of supports and developmental challenges (i.e., psychological stretching). In order to grow, adults need *both* supports and challenges—in general, but also in relation to feedback. An understanding of ways of knowing can help educators intentionally *differentiate* the feedback supports and challenges they offer, since what will feel supportive and challenging isn't the same for everyone. This kind of differentiation lies at the heart of feedback for growth.

Ways of Knowing and Feedback

It can be helpful to think of adults' different ways of knowing as the lenses—or filters—through which they interpret their worlds, as they fundamentally influence how they make sense of and experience their professional commitments, responsibilities, and relationships. In terms of feedback, it can be equally helpful to think of ways of knowing as the *audio frequencies* with which adults transmit and receive information (Drago-Severson & Blum-DeStefano, 2016, 2018). What feedback styles do they *tune into*? What styles push them to *tune out*?

Constructive-developmental theory outlines four distinct ways of knowing more common in adulthood (i.e., instrumental, socializing, self-authoring, and self-transforming). It is important to understand that these are not fixed categories or labels, but rather pause points along an expanding continuum of meaning making. Likewise, ways of knowing are not correlated with kindness, personality style, or intelligence—and each has both strengths and limitations. Put another way, growing into a new way of knowing doesn't make someone a "better" person. Rather, it gives them more internal tools and capacities to address challenges and opportunities.

In particular, growth from one way of knowing to the next involves increases in one's cognitive, affective, interpersonal, and intrapersonal capacities—another definition for growth. As the next sections detail, zooming in on each way of knowing, and understanding the arc of their trajectory, can help feedback givers and receivers alike pinpoint strengths, growing edges, and just-right developmental scaffolding for feedback.

The Instrumental Way of Knowing: "How Do I Get It Right?"

Adults with an instrumental way of knowing have concrete, right/wrong orientations to education and the world. As such, they can excel at concrete and logistical initiatives, and tend to prefer (as givers and receivers) feedback that provides clear directions and expectations (i.e., rubrics, models). While they can bring deep expertise, commitment, and content knowledge to their teaching and leading, it can be harder for instrumental knowers to look beyond what they see as the "right" way to do things (i.e., "This kind of teaching worked for me, so it should work for everyone").

Because a growing edge for instrumental knowers is more fully taking others' perspectives, feedback that invites them to look beyond right/wrong thinking and to consider different points of view can be a powerful stretch for development.

The Socializing Way of Knowing: "What You Think of Me, I Think of Me"

Adults with a socializing way of knowing *have* developed the capacity to stand in another person's shoes more fully, and can attune well to the relational and interpersonal dimensions of their teaching and professional collaborations. However, because socializing knowers orient strongly to valued others'—and society's—opinions and assessments of them, they can struggle with conflict or difficult conversations.

Accordingly, affirming, supportive feedback feels best to socializing knowers (as both givers and receivers). At the same time, gently modeling conflict and constructive feedback as essential parts of relationships (rather than threats to them) can be a powerful support for growth.

The Self-Authoring Way of Knowing: "Let Me Tell You What I Think"

Growing into a self-authoring way of knowing involves taking more conscious, reflective perspective on others' expectations and feedback—and developing the corresponding internal capacity to generate one's *own* values, standards, and beliefs. While self-authoring knowers can still value their relationships and other people's feelings, what becomes most important for them is teaching, leading, and living in line with their own values and bench of judgment. What can be harder for self-authoring knowers is taking a perspective on that value system (i.e., "How might it still be incomplete?), and/or inviting other into their practice and vision.

Feedback, then, that allows the giver/receiver to recognize or demonstrate competency, autonomy, and expertise tends to be a default "frequency" for self-authoring knowers. Inviting these knowers to begin to take a greater perspective on their self-generated understanding of the "best" way can help open space for further growth and development (i.e., how might even one's most carefully curated and closely held beliefs/ideals not encompass the full picture?).

The Self-Transforming Way of Knowing: "What's Important for Each of Us?"

Like self-authoring knowers, self-transforming knowers have personal value systems and philosophies that they've developed over time, but they are no longer run by them in the psychological sense. Rather, they seek continually to explore new areas for growth and perspective taking through interconnection and mutuality. Feedback that takes a more inquiry-oriented, collaborative approach generally feels most supportive to adults with this way of knowing—while they may need more support turning back toward concrete action and managing some kinds of hierarchical systems.

So, what does all of this mean for supervisors, school leaders and instructional coaches, for example? How might they inquire with teachers to learn about their way of knowing? By listening carefully and caringly—and with developmental intentionality—supervisors, school leaders, and instructional coaches can learn to discern a teacher's way of knowing and tailor feedback in a developmentally appropriate manner.

Asking questions before, during, and after giving feedback can help supervisors and school leaders understand how to differentiate their feedback to teachers. For example, asking questions before giving feedback can give school leaders a sense of approximately how a teacher is making meaning—and what matters most to the individual. For example, some questions to ask before giving feedback follow:

- When you think back on your prior experiences, what kinds of things felt most helpful and supportive to you when receiving feedback?
- Can you help me understand a time when getting feedback worked very well for you? What was that like? What made it a good experience? (Supervisors could also ask the inverse to help understand the teacher's way of knowing.)

After giving feedback, school leaders can—as discussed later in this chapter—check in with a teacher to learn how the feedback session was experienced by the teacher and also ask, "What could I do to make our feedback sessions more meaningful for you?"

Holding Environments: Tuning into Feedback as an Intentionally Developmental Opportunity

As this chapter has begun to explore, when thinking about feedback as an avenue for growth—rather than a means to an end or way to simply get things done—it essential to approach feedback as an intentionally developmental experience, or *holding environment* (Drago-Severson, 2004, 2009, 2012; Drago-Severson & Blum-DeStefano, 2016, 2018; Kegan, 1982, 1994). From a developmental perspective, a holding environment is any a context that authentically meets people where they are and offers an artful blend

Table 3.1. Feedback "frequencies" and growing edges for adults with different ways of knowing

Way of Knowing	Feedback "Tuning in" Frequencies	Growing Edges
Instrumental	• Concrete suggestions • Models, rubrics, and examples • Focus on what went right/wrong	• Looking beyond "right" and "wrong" • Taking others' perspectives • Making abstract connections
Socializing	• Authentic praise, validation, and "glows" • Acknowledgment of personhood and feelings • Care for and appreciation of personal qualities	• Engaging in conflict or difficult conversations • Expressing ideas or feelings that could threaten relationships
Self-authoring	• Recognition/demonstration of competence and expertise • Exploration of own ideas and goals • Thoughtful critique in line with values and vision	• Taking a perspective on own values, ideas, and internally generated philosophies • Seeing possibility in opposing ideas and points of view
Self-transforming	• Mutual reflection • Open-ended discussion • Exploration of alternatives, contradictions, and paradoxes	• Turning back toward action amidst competing options • Navigating hierarchy and the slow pace of change

Source: Adapted from Drago-Severson and Blum-DeStefano (2016).

of both support *and* challenge. People really do need both to grow—and feedback can serve this higher purpose!

More specifically, understanding ways of knowing provides one important way into this essential balance, as further illustrated in Table 3.1. Tuning into the feedback frequencies that feel most comfortable to feedback receivers' ways of knowing will help them really hear and take in key ideas, and offering just-right challenges at people's growing edges can help them not only better accomplish the task at hand but also develop new internal capacities.

A Reflective Moment: Tapping Into Your Experience

Please take a moment to reflect through free writing or free thinking about the following:

1. When was the last time you received feedback that was helpful?
2. What was the context?
3. What was your relationship with the feedback giver?
4. What helped you to take it in?

ADDITIONAL STRATEGIES FOR DEVELOPMENTAL, DIFFERENTIATED FEEDBACK

In addition to thinking carefully and in advance about the developmental supports and stretches most appropriate for a particular feedback conversation, depending upon participants' ways of knowing, there are a number of in-the-moment moves you can make as a feedback giver to further bring these strategies into practice (Drago-Severson & Blum-DeStefano, 2016, 2018):

1. Be transparent
2. Check in
3. Really listen
4. Check out and follow up

Be Transparent

Being transparent about the nature and purpose of your feedback before and at the beginning of a feedback conversation—as well as the professional "hat" you happen to have on at the time (i.e., evaluative, collegial, formal, informal)—can be a great show of respect and also a relief for adults with any way of knowing.

What is your feedback for? Why are you offering it? Through what lens? Supervisors, school leaders, and instructional coaches can address these kinds of questions explicitly before giving feedback. Even, and especially when the feedback ahead may be difficult or sensitive, transparency and honesty—when delivered with authenticity and developmental intentionality—can help show care and investment.

Check In

Inviting colleagues to share their feelings, current thinking, and/or important updates at the start of a feedback meeting or conversation can help you establish a respectful, interpersonal foundation for feedback, and honor the full personhoods of all at the table.

That said, individuals will likely orient differently to invitations to share and connect in professional contexts, so differentiating check-in prompts and opportunities—and/or offering moments for private reflection and grounding—can help adults with different ways of knowing enter most comfortably into feedback conversations. Something as important, powerful, and simple as asking, "How are you today?" can make a tremendous difference in honoring the interpersonal and demonstrating care before engaging in a feedback conversation.

Really Listen

One of the simplest but most profoundly important things a feedback giver can do to support another's development is *join them*—as caringly and as carefully as possible—in their thinking, feeling, and meaning making. People can feel and sense when others are truly with them, and this kind of *focused presence* can in and of itself support development, as it allows you to tune into the frequencies that will feel most supportive and productive for colleagues.

Check Out and Follow Up

Akin to checking in, checking out at the very end of a meeting (as a parallel strategy to checking in) can help all participants gain greater clarity, revisit hopes and expectations, and close well. Indeed, asking questions like, "How are you feeling about our meeting?" "What challenges do you anticipate?" and/or "What kinds of supports might you need?" can help bridge feedback and action by intentionally laying the groundwork for next steps—while offering more clues about necessary developmental supports and challenges.

CONCLUSION

This chapter presented the theoretical underpinnings and practical implications of a developmental approach to differentiating feedback. This approach is one that centers on honoring developmental diversity, in addition to the other forms of diversity educators need to recognize and honor in our world. It can help all of us to listen more deeply and differently, to understand each other in new and important ways, and to meet each other where we are as we strive to build a better world. In this way, feedback really is a kind of feeding forward—and investment in the future, ourselves, and one another.

Educators, supervisors, school leaders, and instructional coaches are living, teaching, learning, and leading in the context of ultimate adaptive challenges. Perhaps more urgently than ever, educators of across levels and in a variety of positions are grappling with profound and unanswered questions—like how to support students, communities, and each other through ongoing racial, educational, social, and economic injustices; through the ever-changing phases of the COVID-19 pandemic; and through reignited political and curriculum debates.

They do this all while aspiring to create, together, futures grounded in growth, transformation, and healing (Drago-Severson et al., 2020; Keating,

2013; Khalifa, 2018; Singleton, 2014). As this chapter has illuminated, a developmental approach to feedback can help with enhancing feedback practices—and thus, can help educators help each other grow, improve instruction, and instructional leadership as they strive to create a better future and world for children in their care.

POSTREADING REFLECTIONS/ACTIVITIES

After reading this chapter, please take a moment to consider the following questions.

- What are implications of a developmental lens on feedback—or pieces of it—for your *personal growth and learning*? What is one next step for you?
- How might the practices and strategies discussed in this chapter apply to working with *those in your care*? What is one next step for you?
- How, if at all, might you share ideas from this chapter to deepen a culture of feedback in your work context?

APPLICATION EXERCISE: BUILDING YOUR DEVELOPMENTAL MUSCLE

Please read the vignettes below.[1]

- With which way(s) of knowing do you think each educator is making meaning? What evidence do you see in the vignettes to support your developmental assessments (knowing you are seeing just a glimpse of each person's meaning making)?
- What seems to be a growing edge—in the developmental sense—for each educator? What might be a helpful developmental support for each person based on where they currently seem to be in their meaning making and practice?
- What kind of feedback might feel supportive to each educator? Challenging in a growth-oriented way?

Quinn

I always wanted to be a teacher. I guess I just wanted to do something good—to be a good person, you know? And I did everything right. I studied hard, got good grades, took all the courses I needed for my certification, and got an almost perfect score on my state test. I was ready to change the world!

When I got my first job, I was so happy. Like other new teachers in the building, I spent weeks before the start of school in my classroom planning my lessons and getting my bulletin board just right. I also memorized all my kids' names from the roster. Everything was in order, and I was ready. So, you could imagine my shock when nothing worked! Like, nothing. *I couldn't get through a lesson. My kids couldn't care less about the material or me or all the things we were supposed to be doing.*

I was staying later and later each day, searching Google for new ideas, rereading my old notes and study guides, and pretty much barely sleeping trying to figure it all out. I knew there was an answer, but I was missing it somehow. What was I doing wrong?

I don't think I could have made it through that first year without Sarah and Liam, the other teachers on my sixth-grade team. Sarah's just, like, so wise, you know? And Liam has this way with the kids that just amazes me. They really embraced me—gave me tips and pointers, listened to me vent, and even invited me out after work sometimes. It helps so much to have people around me who know the kinds of things that fly in our school. I'd really be lost without them.

Pey

In the years we've worked together, Nami, my principal, has done so much for me. She helps me with my lessons, answers all *of my questions, and gives me the best suggestions after observations. She even listens to my family problems. Honestly, she's brilliant, and her vision for the school has made a tremendous difference. Her friendship means the world to me, too.*

Lately, though, I've been struggling with something. I've been taking on more and more for Nami. I'm organizing the back-to-school picnic and the homecoming dance, mentoring three new teachers, and giving up a prep period twice a week to cover an extra class; all because she asked me to. I know I need to say something, but I'm just not sure how. I can't quite imagine telling Nami "no," but I really can't do all of this anymore. When I think about becoming a principal, I realize I need to develop a better sense of who I am as a leader so I can be more comfortable leading others.

Amal

I started the School for Change five years ago and now, every morning, I get to walk into a school building that's, well, bustling with learning. Kids are doing collaborative projects in multiage classrooms. Co-teachers are leading every classroom community together. We've infused the arts and culturally responsive pedagogy into our major subject curricula, and I'm on cloud nine.

Now, don't get me wrong—this stuff is very hard. I personally hire and train every teacher who joins the team, and I do all of the observations and have a hand in most of the PD. For the most part, my staff is right there with me. And they know that if they're not on board with the mission, it's time to get off the bus, so to speak.

I have been thinking more lately, though, about how to encourage teachers to stay at the school longer. During an exit interview recently, one of my veteran teachers—who decided to take a new job—shared something that really stuck with me. "Amal," she said, "I know this school is your baby, and that your mission is really clear, but you work so hard to make sure the kids and all of us teachers are collaborating, and then do everything by yourself. *I'm not sure I have anything left to offer here." That was really hard to hear—this was a really super-star teacher—but there was something so important about what she said.*

NOTE

1. Adapted from Drago-Severson & Blum-DeStefano (2018).

REFERENCES

Boudett, K. P., City, E. A., & Murnane, R. J. (Eds.). (2005). *Data wise: A step-by-step guide to using assessment data results to improve teaching and learning.* Harvard Education Press.

Danielson, C. (December 2010/January 2011). Evaluations that help teachers learn. *Education Leadership, 68*(4), 35–39.

Drago-Severson, E. (2004). *Helping teachers learn: Principal leadership for adult growth and development.* Corwin/Sage.

Drago-Severson, E. (2009). *Leading adult learning: Supporting adult development in our schools.* Corwin/Sage and Learning Forward.

Drago-Severson, E. (2012). *Helping educators grow: Strategies and practices for leadership development.* Harvard Education Press.

Drago-Severson, E., & Blum-DeStefano, J. (2016). *Tell me so I can hear you: A developmental approach to feedback for educators.* Harvard Education Press.

Drago-Severson, E., & Blum-DeStefano, J. (2018). *Leading change together: Developing educator capacity within schools and systems.* ASCD.

Drago-Severson, E., Blum-DeStefano, J., & Brooks Lawrence, D. (2020). Connections bring us Closer to equity and justice. *The Learning Professional, 41*(5).

Hallinger, P., Heck, R. H., & Murphy, J. (2014). Teacher evaluation and school improvement: An analysis. *Educational Assessment, Evaluation and Accountability, 26*(1), 1–24.

Harris, D. N., Ingle, W. K., & Rutledge, S. A. (2014). How teacher evaluation methods matter in accountability: A comparative analysis of teacher effectiveness ratings by principals and teacher value-added measures. *American Educational Research Journal, 51*(1), 73–112.

Keating, A. (2013). *Transformation now! Toward a post-oppositional politics of change.* University of Illinois Press.

Kegan, R. (1982). *The evolving self: Problem and process in human development.* Harvard University Press.

Kegan, R. (1994). *In over our heads: The mental demands of modern life.* Harvard University Press.

Khalifa, M. (2018). *Culturally responsive leadership.* Harvard Education Press.

Lavigne, A. L., & Good, T. L. (2013). *Teacher and student evaluation: Moving beyond the failure of school reform.* Routledge.

MacDonald, E. (June 2011). When nice won't suffice: Honest discourse is key to shifting school culture. *Journal of Staff Development, 32*(3), 45–47, 51.

Marshall, K. (2013). *Rethinking teacher supervision and evaluation: How to work smart, build collaboration, and close the achievement gap* (2nd ed.). John Wiley & Sons.

Singleton, G. (2014). *Courageous conversations about race: A field guide for achieving equity in schools* (2nd ed.). Corwin.

Stone, D., & Heen, S. (2015). *Thanks for the feedback: The science and art of receiving feedback well.* Penguin.

CHAPTER 4

A Strategic Human Resource Orientation to Teacher Supervision

Melissa Tuytens, Eva Vekeman, and Geert Devos

PREFOCUS GUIDING QUESTIONS

- How can teacher supervision contribute to achieve school goals (strategic orientation)?
- How can teacher supervision contribute to meet teachers' individual needs (human resource orientation)?
- Can schools achieve a balanced approach to teacher supervision, taking into account both a strategic orientation and a human resource orientation?
- What are hampering factors in the internal and external school context to engage in effective teacher supervision?
- What are aiding factors in the internal and external school context to engage in effective teacher supervision?

INTRODUCTION

Within schools, teachers are central as resources to provide quality education. This implies that schools should invest in teachers and their development. Strategic human resource management (SHRM) can contribute to this goal (Leisink & Boselie, 2014). SHRM is an approach of personnel policies and practices that focuses on the importance of aligning these policies and practices to both the strategical planning of the organization (i.e., strategic orientation) as well as to the individual needs of employees within the organization (i.e., human resource orientation; Tuytens et al., 2021).

One of the important personnel practices in education consists of teacher supervision, which can be seen as "a career-long continuum of practice that fosters teacher growth while ensuring quality teaching" (Brandon et al., 2018,

p. 264). Teacher supervision, as a personnel practice, also benefits from a balanced approach by paying attention to both a strategic and human resource orientation. As Stronge (2006) emphasized, individual and institutional goals are intertwined in the context of teacher supervision and, hence, teacher supervision should be used to aim for individual and school improvement.

Although there is consensus in the literature on this point, research also shows that schools are struggling with teacher supervision and this broad focus on both teacher and school improvement (Darling-Hammond, 2015). Research shows, for example, that concerning teacher supervision, principals seem to prioritize human resource approaches that focus on the needs of individuals within the organization over more structural approaches that focus on objective procedures and goal-oriented work of organizational structures (Campbell & Derrington, 2019).

Also, considering that schools do not operate in a vacuum (Leisink & Boselie, 2014), internal and external context variables should be considered as influential for personnel policies and practices, such as teacher supervision (Paauwe, 2004). A review study regarding teacher supervision showed that there is a lack of research regarding context variables that are influential for teacher supervision in schools (Tuytens et al., 2020). This review found few studies focusing on external context variables, such as institutional variables either specific to the education context (e.g., legislation, unions) or specific to the culture of a country.

A bit more frequently—however, still sparsely—school internal context variables in the context of teacher supervision were investigated, such as school size and the role of time. This lack of research to identify influential context variables for teacher supervision is problematic as it hinders us in understanding the contextual conditions for teacher supervision to foster positive results for the school and teachers.

After all, the conclusion that an intervention in a specific context leads to positive results will not necessarily be true in another context (Ton et al., 2011). To counter these limited findings regarding context, several authors (e.g., Flores & Derrington, 2017; Tuytens et al., 2020) recommend the further investigation of the role of context variables for supervision.

This chapter unravels the current state of affairs regarding the balanced approach (i.e., combining a strategic and human resource orientation) of teacher supervision in primary and secondary schools and to understand why schools are struggling to implement this balanced approach. Therefore, this chapter will also elaborate on hampering or aiding context variables for strategic and human resource-oriented teacher supervision. Furthermore, the chapter zooms in on the outcomes for teachers in schools in which the balanced approach is reached. More concretely, we focus on teacher well-being and teachers' learning goal orientation.

This qualitative study was carried out in 12 primary and 12 secondary schools in Flanders, Belgium. The data collection for this study lasted an entire school year and consisted of 194 interviews with school leaders (principals, assistant principals, etc.) and teachers (minimum of three teachers per school), document analyses, and observations of several staff meetings. Based on these data, we performed vertical and horizontal qualitative analyses to gain insights in the teacher supervision practice in schools through diverse perspectives.

In Flanders (Belgium), teacher supervision is obligatory in schools. All Flemish teachers should receive a job description that contains clear expectations regarding teacher work in the school. For the majority of Flemish teachers, teacher supervision focuses on a formative process in which a teacher is provided with regular feedback during feedback conversations. These feedback conversations are held by a school leader (principal or vice principal) and focus on coaching and professional growth of the teacher.

Next to these formative feedback conversations, additional summative evaluation conversations are possible. However, these are only used for certain groups of teachers (e.g., ill-functioning teachers or beginning, non-tenured teachers). In the case of a summative evaluation conversation, an evaluation report is handed to the teacher with a final (negative or positive) conclusion (Department of Education, 2007).

Defining a Strategic Human Resource Orientation to Teacher Supervision

Above, taking into account both a strategic and a human resource orientation, we described how a balanced approach to teacher supervision is beneficial for the practice in schools. In this regard, it is also important to define this balanced approach to teacher supervision and to present a clear conceptualization of this balanced approach. In line with other authors (e.g., Derrington & Martinez, 2019; Runhaar, 2017), we define teacher supervision in our study as a process with both formative and summative objectives. In essence, it holds teachers accountable, but it is also a means to improve teachers' practice.

Both objectives require accurate assessments of teachers' performance based on a clear description of teacher standards. Applying the balanced approach to teacher supervision leads to the following categories used in our study to determine whether teacher supervision put in practice in schools is strategic and human resource oriented:

- 0 – teacher supervision is not aligned with strategic planning nor individual needs of teachers (i.e., "totally unbalanced"). There are generic

classroom visits and feedback conversations with teachers based on standard teacher performance criteria.
- 0.5 – teacher supervision is aligned with strategic planning or individual needs of teachers (i.e., "unbalanced because of a unilateral approach"). There are classroom visits and feedback conversations with teachers in which the strategic plan of the school or individual needs are put forward as foci.
- 1 – teacher supervision is aligned with strategic planning and individual needs of teachers (i.e., "balanced approach"). There are classroom visits and feedback conversations with teachers in which the strategic plan of the school and individual needs is put forward as foci.

Within this chapter, we see schools with a score 1 for teacher supervision as schools with a balanced approach. Schools that score 0 or 0.5 are considered as schools with an unbalanced approach to teacher supervision.

Realizing a Strategic Human Resource Orientation to Teacher Supervision

If we zoom in on how teachers are supervised in the Flemish schools in our study, our data shows that 12 out of 24 schools (i.e., seven elementary schools and five secondary schools) can be identified as *schools with a balanced approach to teacher supervision*. These schools invest in classroom visits and feedback conversations in which both strategic planning of the school and teachers' individual needs are taken into account. This is realized by providing teachers a clear format for both classroom visits and feedback conversations.

In these schools, we also observe that classroom visits and feedback conversations are regularly performed with teachers. There is also a clear communication with teachers about the teacher supervision procedure. In feedback conversations, feedback is given that is clearly related to aspects of the school's strategic planning as well as to aspects of teachers' personal development plan.

Also, all teachers in the school are part of the teacher supervision procedure, albeit classroom visits and feedback conversations with experienced teachers take place less frequently than with beginning teachers. The following quote from the principal of D illustrates the balanced approach in which both school goals and teacher needs are addressed.

> When I look at last school year, what was the focus? These are things we have taken from our strategic development plan. . . . Last year the focus was interactive reading to toddlers . . . . We made agreements about the processing of this reading in small groups. Then I plan classroom observations. . . . Afterwards I reflect on the observation with the teacher. My first question is also, "What

did you experience as a strong point?" This is always very difficult for teachers. Then we look for growth opportunities and then we search for solutions together. . . . Last year I visited everyone and made a report on that. I perceive these pedagogical and didactical aspects as a basis on which the performance appraisal conversation can start. (Principal, school D)

Certain schools in our sample, used the "hand-methodology" as a guide for feedback conversations (see appendix 4.1). This methodology encourages a balanced approach for teacher supervision as is explained by the principal of school D:

Using the hand-methodology, so the five fingers. . . . Questions like: "How can I support you? What can I do different? Do you think your talents are being appreciated? . . . And then also regarding the future: do you want to invest in innovative education? As a school, we stand for "workshops," what's your vision as a teacher? We do discuss this individually with the teachers.

In our data, four schools (i.e., two elementary schools and two secondary schools) were identified as *unbalanced because of a unilateral approach*. This implies that there is no balanced approach, but a unilateral approach focusing only on strategic planning *or* teacher individual needs through teacher supervision.

In our data, all partial strategic schools focused unilaterally on teacher individual needs instead of strategic planning. This means that in most of these schools, classroom visits and feedback conversations are carried out where the principals focus on a formative evaluation of teachers' personal development plan both for beginning and experienced teachers. The following quote from the principal of school 4 illustrates the unbalanced, unilateral approach merely on teacher needs:

Mainly we aim with a performance appraisal conversation to ask the teacher "How do you feel?"; "Which expectations do you have?"; "What do you want to talk about?" (Principal, school 4)

Finally, eight schools (i.e., four elementary schools and four secondary schools) in our sample were identified as *totally unbalanced* for teacher supervision. In these schools, no classroom visits nor feedback conversations take place on a regular basis. This also implies that no balanced approach or even a unilateral approach could be identified at the time of the research. The following quote from a teacher in school J illustrates this totally unbalanced approach by pointing out that there is no investment in feedback conversations in the school, not even when requested by the teacher:

No, up to now I never had a performance appraisal conversation. I asked for it myself: "[name principal], can I have a performance appraisal conversation?

I'm here already for two years. . . ." It is not too soon, no? . . . Sometimes I think, "Come on, just take a look in my classroom?" (Teacher, school J)

In these schools with an unbalanced approach, teacher supervision seems to occur only for dysfunctional teachers or (mostly beginning) teachers are supervised in a formal way based on general standards only in order to comply with the legislation. One principal explains why not more effort is put in teacher supervision:

> It is not possible to do that [teacher supervision]. I do the necessary. . . . I don't need to go in teachers' classroom and say, "How are you doing here?" I know how they work. I see the results [of pupils]. You listen to parents, to the environment, . . . You know that's going well. (Principal, school I)

Hampering and Aiding Factors for a Balanced Approach for Teacher Supervision

As indicated above, schools do not operate in a vacuum. Hence, it is important to take into account the role of context variables, which influence teacher supervision approaches in schools. During interviews with school principals, we asked which context factors were hampering or aiding for the teacher supervision approach in the schools. Two aiding factors related to the school board and three hampering factors were mentioned by school principals (see figure 4.1).

Autonomy by School Board

Considering teacher supervision, principals (of one elementary school and three secondary schools) mention to appreciate the autonomy they receive of the school board. In Flanders, the school board is the official

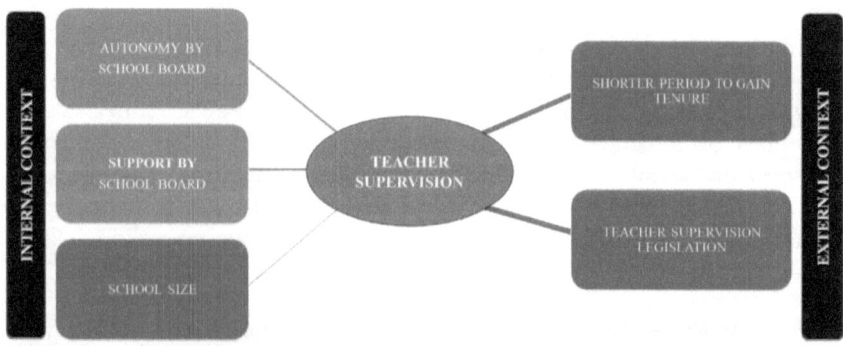

Figure 4.1. Summarizing scheme aiding/hampering context factors for teacher supervision

employer of teachers. However, the school principal is the main supervisor of teachers. If school principals feel they can perform teacher supervision autonomously without interference of the school board, they appreciate this autonomy:

> You need to receive trust: "Principal, you will take care of it in your school." I find that very important. That autonomy. "It is your school: go ahead." (Principal, school 6)

Support by School Board

We notice that for principals in four schools, the support of their school board for teacher supervision seems to be important. This is mainly related to the support school leaders experience when there are complaints about teacher supervision from teachers. For three principals, the importance of this support goes hand in hand with the autonomy they receive of the school board:

> We have very high autonomy. Unless there is a conflict and they have to mediate. They do that really well. You get support from all sides. That is no problem. . . . They said at a certain time: "We trust you! Make sure you can explain why you proceeded a certain way, and we don't need to know more." (Principal, school 5)

School Size

Several school leaders indicate that the number of teachers that must be supervised can be a problem. One secondary school, not by coincidence the largest one in our sample, mentions school size explicitly as a hampering factor for teacher supervision. Although the school involves every leadership team member that can officially be a teacher supervisor, they still have the experience where the number of teachers to be supervised per supervisor is too large.

> Well, we do have large groups of teachers. I have 40 teachers [of which I'm the supervisor]. So, it is a matter of trying to see everybody a couple of times. It barely works out. I did finish the cycle with five, six teachers. That means two feedback conversations and one evaluation conference in four years' time. But for the others, I did not succeed. (Principal, school 4)

Shorter Period to Gain Tenure

From September 2019 onward, the rules regarding tenure changed in Flanders. Before this date, teachers had to work at least 600 days in one school network to gain a more fixed contract in the schools of that school network. This period shortened in September 2019 to 400 days. At that point, the supervisor of the teacher can provide an evaluation of the performance of the teacher. When there is no explicit negative evaluation of the teacher, the teacher gains the right to have a more fixed contract the next school year.

The majority of principals in our sample is not favoring this new legislation. Nine principals (three in elementary and six in secondary schools) mention that this hampers the quality of teacher supervision. They feel it is not feasible as a supervisor to be able to thoroughly evaluate a teacher based on 400 days of performance in the school (or school network).

> Sometimes in the first year, they have scattered assignments which doesn't allow you to properly evaluate them. You don't have time to give them give them feedback to improve. . . . It is difficult to decide in such a short time period. You are stuck with them if it is not okay. (Principal, school K)

Teacher Supervision Legislation

Mainly, in secondary education, principals find the legislation for teacher supervision hampering. Nine secondary school leaders mention this. Only one elementary school leader also mentions this explicitly. The main argument that school leaders cite is the long and difficult procedure for a negative evaluation after the teacher supervision procedure.

> We resign ourselves that we don't give negative evaluations. We had two teachers who could have been negatively evaluated, but they were at the end of their career. We don't do that. We try to coach, but to make a whole procedure out of it. No, we don't do that. There is no point. Then you only send one another to the legal procedure and in the end, you have a hard time proving things. (Principal, school 10)

In this regard, school leaders choose to mainly focus on formative conversations with teachers in which they provide feedback. They find this useful and important, but often they choose not to evaluate teachers in a formal way for efficiency reasons.

> The difference between a formative and a summative conversation, I still have difficulties to see that difference. For me, it is about the conversation itself and the motivation to aim higher. (Principal, school 5)

What's in it for the Teacher?

Six school leaders explicitly refer to the practice of teacher supervision to stimulate teacher well-being. In line with other researchers (e.g., Engels et al., 2004; Van Petegem et al., 2005), we define teachers' well-being as a positive emotional state that is the result of a harmony between the sum of specific context factors on the one hand and the personal needs and expectations toward the school on the other hand. This definition refers to a kind of harmony between the person and the school which means we look at well-being of teaching within a specific school.

We observe that principals in schools with a balanced approach to teacher supervision mention more often (four principals) that they aim to stimulate teacher well-being in comparison to principals in schools with an unbalanced approach to teacher supervision (two principals).

> I experience that during a performance appraisal conversation a lot of personal issues are discussed. Teachers like it that you listen to them. . . . That is beneficial for the relationship between teachers and the principal but it also gives a perspective on teachers' well-being. (Principal, school 1)

During teacher interviews, we also asked teachers how they perceive their own well-being in the school. We considered teachers' well-being as high when the teacher referred in general to positive emotions about teaching in the school.

When we look at the results (table 4.1) related to teacher well-being in school with a balanced approach to teacher supervision, we notice that on

Table 4.1. Percentage of teachers with high well-being in schools with a balanced approach to teacher supervision versus schools with an unbalanced approach to teacher supervision

Schools with Balanced Approach in Teacher Supervision (12)	CASE	Percentage of Teachers with High Well-Being	Schools without Balanced Approach in Supervision (12)	CASE	Percentage of Teachers with High Well-Being
Primary schools (7)	A	83.3%	Primary schools (5)	C	66.7%
	B	75%		H	100%
	D	66.7%		I	66.7%
	E	33.3%		J	33.3%
	F	100%		K	33.3%
	G	33.3%			
	L	66.7%			
Secondary schools (5)	3	100%	Secondary schools (7)	1	80%
	7	66.7%		2	75%
	8	100%		4	100%
	9	100%		5	75%
	12	100%		6	66.7%
				10	40%
				11	100%
Average total		*77.1 %*	*Average total*		*69.7%*

average 77.1 percent of the teachers reported a high well-being. This average percentage was a bit lower (69.7 percent) in schools with an unbalanced approach of teacher supervision. When looking more closely at the results in table 4.1, it is striking to see that, especially in secondary education, a balanced approach to teacher supervision seems to contribute to teacher well-being.

In this regard, we think that in secondary schools, which are larger than primary schools in Flanders (Belgium), teacher supervision provides formal opportunities to the teacher to have a conversation about their practice with a school principal, which is less obvious in an informal manner (e.g., an informal chat) than in smaller, primary schools. Related to this, we also feel that a balanced approach to teacher supervision ensures that both the organizational and the individual needs are addressed during teacher supervision and this seems to contribute to the well-being of teachers.

A second teacher outcome that we consider in this study is teachers' learning-goal orientation. The learning-goal orientation refers to teachers' motivation to continuously improve one's competencies through learning and training new skills, as well as through learning to complete new and more complex tasks (Dweck & Legett, 1988).

When teachers have a high learning-goal orientation, they are motivated to learn. This means, for example, that they are likely to view activities like asking for feedback, letting others observe their teaching and experimenting with new teaching methods as challenging ways to grow rather than as activities that may affect their self-image (Runhaar, 2017).

In this study, we considered teachers' learning orientation in a school as high when respondents in the school perceive that, within the school, teachers in general are strongly motivated to learn professionally.

We noticed (see table 4.2) that the majority of schools with a balanced approach to teacher supervision also demonstrated high teachers' learning-goal orientation (nine schools). In this regard, we believe this indicates

Table 4.2. Number of schools with high and low perception on teachers' learning orientation within the school in schools with a balanced approach to teacher supervision versus schools with an unbalanced approach

	Teachers' Learning Goal Orientation within the School	Cases
High	**13 (54.2%)**	
Schools with balanced approach	9	A, B, D, E, F, G, 3, 8, 9
Schools with unbalanced approach	4	J, 2, 6, 11
Low	**11 (45.8%)**	
Schools with balanced approach	2	7, 12
Schools with unbalanced approach	9	C, H, I, K, L, 1, 4, 5, 10
Total	24 (100%)	

that the willingness to learn for example from feedback during teacher supervision seems to be more optimal here than in schools with an unbalanced-teacher-supervision approach.

CONCLUSION

In this chapter, we described the importance of a balanced approach to teacher supervision in which both an orientation on the strategic planning of the school and a human resource orientation that focuses on teachers' individual needs are united. We notice that half of the schools in our sample succeed in such a balanced approach to teacher supervision. From an optimistic viewpoint, we conclude that this means that a balanced approach is achievable in school practice. From a more pessimistic viewpoint, we can conclude that schools seem to struggle with such a balanced approach.

In a next section, we also identified which school context factors are influential for achieving a strategic human resource-oriented approach. We focused here on the role of school boards to give autonomy and support to schools for teacher supervision. Also, we notice that certain context variables which schools themselves cannot influence are important (such as school size and legislation).

Lastly, we showed that a balanced approach to teacher supervision might be related to teacher well-being and teachers' learning-goal orientation. Although we feel our study provides interesting first insights into a strategic human-oriented approach to teacher supervision, we also want to acknowledge the exploratory character of our study in a small sample of schools.

Hence, we want to encourage both researchers and school practitioners to further explore the strategic human-resource approach to teacher supervision, the influence of context for this approach, and its relation to outcomes. We certainly encourage to further share insights about the strategic human resource approach to teacher supervision.

POSTREADING REFLECTIONS/ACTIVITIES

- In this chapter, we conclude that a balanced approach (i.e., paying attention to school goals [strategic orientation] and individual needs [human resource orientation]) in teacher supervision is achievable in school practice. What do you think? In your opinion, what might help school leaders in balancing school goals and individual needs?
- In which way does the teacher-supervision legislation in your country hampers school leaders in paying attention to a balanced approach? Which expectations formulated in the teacher-supervision legislation could be handled in a more efficient and less bureaucratic way?

- In which way does the school board support school leaders in teacher supervision? How might school board provide more support for school leaders?
  - Is supervision only a task of the school leader? Who else within the school might be involved in teacher supervision?
  - How can teacher supervision stimulate teacher well-being and teachers' learning-goal orientation in your school?

REFERENCES

Brandon, J., Hollweck, T., Donlevy, J. K., & Whalen, C. (2018). Teacher supervision and evaluation challenges: Canadian perspectives on overall instructional leadership. *Teachers and Teaching, 24*(3), 263–80. https://doi.org/10.1080/13540602.2018.1425678

Campbell, J. W., & Derrington, M. (2019). Principals' perceptions of teacher evaluation reform from structural and human resource perspectives. *Journal of Educational Supervision, 2*(1), 58–77. https://doi.org/10.31045/jes.2.1.4

Darling-Hammond, L. (2015). *Getting teacher evaluation right: What really matters for effectiveness and improvement.* Teachers College Press.

Department of Education. (2007). *Omzendbrief omtrent functiebeschrijving en evaluatie [Letter to the schools about job descriptions and evaluation].* Flemish Ministry of Education.

Derrington, M. L., & Martinez, J. A. (2019). Exploring teachers' evaluation perceptions: A snapshot. *NASSP Bulletin, 103*(1), 32–50. https://doi.org/10.1177%2F0192636519830770

Dweck, C. S., & Legett, E. L. (1988). A social cognitive approach to motivation and personality. *Psychological Review, 95*(2), 256–73. https://psycnet.apa.org/doi/10.1037/0033-295X.95.2.256

Engels, N., Aelterman, A., Van Petegem, K., & Schepens, A. (2004). Factors which influence the well-being of pupils in Flemish secondary schools. *Educational Studies, 30*(2), 127–43. https://doi.org/10.1080/0305569032000159787

Flores, M. A., & Derrington, M. L. (2017). School principals' views of teacher evaluation policy: Lessons learned from two empirical studies. *International Journal of Leadership in Education, 20*(4), 416–31. https://doi.org/10.1080/13603124.2015.1094144

Leisink, P., & Boselie, P. (2014). *Strategisch HRM voor beter onderwijs: Een bijdrage aan de professionalisering van schoolleiders in het voorgezet onderwijs* [Strategic HRM for better education. A contribution to principals' professional development in secondary education]. Departement voor Bestuurs- en Organisatiewetenschap (USBO), Universiteit Utrecht.

Paauwe, J. (2004). *HRM and performance: Achieving long term validity.* Oxford University Press.

Runhaar, P. (2017). How can schools and teachers benefit from human resources management? Conceptualising HRM from content and process perspectives.

Educational Management Administration & Leadership, 45(4), 639–56. https://doi.org/10.1177%2F1741143215623786

Stronge, J. H. (2006). Teacher evaluation and school improvement: Improving the educational landscape. *Evaluating teaching: A guide to current thinking and best practice, 2*, 1–23. https://dx.doi.org/10.4135/9781412990202.d4

Ton, G., Vellema, S., & De Ruyter De Wildt, M. (2011). Development impacts of value chain interventions: How to collect credible evidence and draw valid conclusions in impact evaluations? *Journal on Chain and Network Science, 11*(1), 69–84. https://doi.org/10.3920/JCNS2011.x188

Tuytens, M., Devos, G., & Vanblaere, B. (2020). An integral perspective on teacher evaluation: a review of empirical studies. *Educational Assessment Evaluation and Accountability, 32*, 153–83. https://doi.org/10.1007/s11092-020-09321-z

Tuytens, M., Vekeman, E., & Devos, G. (2021). Strategic human resource management in primary and secondary schools. An explorative study in Flanders (Belgium). *Educational Management Administration & Leadership.* Advance online publication. https://doi.org/10.1177%2F1741143221998706

Van Petegem, K., Creemers, B. P. M., Rosseel, Y., & Aelterman, A. (2005). Relationships between teacher characteristics, interpersonal teacher behaviour and teacher well-being. *The Journal of Classroom Interaction, 40*(2), 34–43.

APPENDIX 4.1. THE HAND-METHODOLOGY FOR FEEDBACK CONVERSATIONS

This methodology uses the image of a hand as a guide for feedback conversations and takes into account both a strategic and a human resource orientation:

- The thumb is used as a symbol to express what is appreciated in the functioning of the teacher and the school: What are top moments as experienced by the teacher and the supervisor?
- The index finger symbolizes the direction that both the school and the teacher want to follow and how this can be supported by the school: What does the supervisor/teacher wants to see more in the future?
- The middle finger points out the changes that the school and the teacher want to make in the future: What changes does the supervisor/teacher want to strive for?
- The ring finger expresses the vision that the school and the teacher stand for and is a starting point to discuss whether school and teacher share a mutual vision: What is the vision of the school and the teacher?
- The little finger symbolizes the developmental needs of both the school and the teacher: What does the teacher need to develop professionally in the future?

Source: Broeckaert, R. (2016). *Dienend leidinggeven: zacht voor mensen hard voor resultaten.* [*Servant leadership: soft for people hard for results*] Lannoo Meulenhoff-Belgium.

CHAPTER 5

The Use of Video Analysis in Supervision

Valerie Johnson and Benterah C. Morton

PREFOCUS GUIDING QUESTIONS

- In what ways does the use of video analysis influence school leaders' instructional feedback to teachers?
- In what ways does the use of video analysis assist teachers in becoming more effective?
- What processes can supervisors put into place to successfully implement the use of video analysis and instructional feedback?

INTRODUCTION

The work of educators is complex and difficult, and since the COVID-19 pandemic, the work has become even harder. The challenges seem insurmountable, yet educators must rise to the challenge because students deserve to have effective teachers during every year of their educational experience. How can school and district leaders promote and support effective teaching that will positively impact student learning and achievement? There is myriad research and strategies that purport to increase student achievement, yet school and district leaders must find practical and effective strategies that actually work.

The authors of this chapter encourage educators to utilize video analysis and an instructional feedback cycle to assist teachers in becoming more effective. The chapter explores how the use of video analysis and engagement in the instructional feedback cycle can influence teachers' efficacy beliefs and decision making. Further, it examines methods for school administrators to positively impact teachers' instruction by increasing their sense of efficacy. Finally, this chapter will discuss findings showing that a school principal served as a catalyst in leading changes in teachers' instruction through video analysis.

SCHOOL PRINCIPALS AS LEADERS OF CHANGE

To ensure that students can achieve, it is important that teachers are effective and have the resources and abilities to help students learn at high rates (Hattie, 2009). Both formative and summative evaluations designed to provide teachers with focused feedback may have positive lasting impacts on teacher practices and behaviors and on student achievement. With the increased focus on students' achievement scores, all educators in a school must prove that what they are doing is effective and has a high impact on students' educational success.

The role of the school principal has changed dramatically in recent years and now requires principals to be instructional leaders with the ability to lead efforts to significantly improve student learning and achievement (Morton & Upton, 2020). As a result of this changing role, school leaders (i.e., principals, district leaders, and instructional coaches) must be equipped to deliver detailed and timely feedback to teachers.

The use of video can assist administrators and teachers in observing the same reality and working together to improve instruction (Knight, 2014b). Principal feedback is key to instructional effectiveness and student learning, and coupled with targeted recommendations, this feedback has the potential to improve teacher practice, promote teacher collaboration, and improve both individual and collective teacher efficacy.

IMPACT OF THE USE OF VIDEO ANALYSIS FOR TEACHING AND LEARNING

In an effort to improve teaching and learning, one method that holds promise is the use of video analysis. Since the 1970s, this method has evolved into one that encourages educators to become more reflective in their practice and enables them to critically consider the effects of specific actions within the classroom environment. Previous studies have consistently noted the impact that video analysis can have on helping teachers reflect on their instruction. These impacts include influencing the change process for teachers, empowering teachers to self-diagnose problems, and assisting them in prescribing effective strategies for student learning.

In practical application, video analysis helps teachers notice things about their instruction that they did not remember while teaching, and they gain a better ability to assess their own strengths and weaknesses. Video analysis can give teachers a crystal-clear picture of true reality, and as a result, they can set specific, student-focused goals (Knight, 2018). Knight discusses the positive impact that video cameras have on teaching and learning while also noting the importance of an implementation that honors teachers' professionalism and learning (Knight, 2014a).

One example of video analysis being used to positively impact teaching and learning is National Board Certification, a process through which teachers can utilize video analysis to improve teaching and learning. The National Board for Professional Teaching Standards (NBPTS) encourages teachers to deeply analyze and reflect on their planning and implementation of instruction and assessment through the lens of their Standards (NBPTS, n.d.).

Throughout the National Board process, educators defend how and why they teach through video analysis and reflection. It is a thought-provoking and reflective process that empowers teachers to move forward in their application of impacting student learning.

In similar fashion, school principals have used video with teacher evaluations and discovered that by using video as part of the dialogue between teachers and principals, they can have a professional and rich conversation regarding the specifics of the teacher's instruction and students' learning interactions (Knight, 2014a). The use of video allows the teacher and administrator to have a clear picture of reality and to have a meaningful discussion about next steps. Finally, the use of video and videoconferencing offers teachers and administrators flexibility in determining when they want to watch the video.

THE USE OF INSTRUCTIONAL FEEDBACK WITH VIDEO ANALYSIS

Because of the ongoing heightened focus on high stakes testing, principals have become the nexus of accountability, and they are expected to function as instructional leaders. Consequently, teachers' evaluations have become a dominant part of the discussion in recent years. However, there is an often absence of feedback that teachers can use to facilitate professional growth geared toward instructional improvement (Balyer & Ozcan, 2020).

The feedback cycle can be greatly beneficial and is "among the most powerful influences on how people learn" (Hattie, 2012, p. 18). The importance of giving and receiving quality feedback that positively impacts teaching and learning cannot be underestimated. Yet, for improvement to occur, school leaders must have the ability to provide constructive and targeted feedback that will improve instruction.

An approach that holds the possibility to disrupt supervisors' typical domination of observation feedback lies in the connection of research between supervisory conferencing and the use of video analysis in teacher development. This connection is a persistent dilemma for supervisors because they must simultaneously adopt two stances: serving as evaluators of performance (summative evaluation) and coaching (formative evaluation) for that performance. This paradox can lead to tensions that play out in postobservation conferences.

To alleviate these tensions, video analysis can be employed as a formative evaluation and resource for educators who want to improve their pedagogical knowledge base, observational skills, and assessment abilities. If school and district leaders implement the video analysis and instructional feedback process for both formative and summative evaluations, it has the capacity to go beyond a relatively limited and somewhat subjective process by providing educators with a tool to assist them in becoming truly reflective practitioners (Baecher & McCormack, 2014).

IMPLEMENTATION OF VIDEO ANALYSIS

The findings and implications presented in this chapter are based on a study using qualitative methodologies. The participants were educators in a rural elementary school in the southeastern United States. Qualitative data for the study was collected through feedback sessions and focus group sessions. Video-based observations of the participants were recorded to collect fine-grained data and evidence of various instructional techniques and strategies. Each teacher met with the principal three times during the course of the research to discuss how each teacher could become more effective by utilizing the Impact Cycle (Knight, 2018).

An instructional feedback cycle between each teacher and the principal occurred to serve as a tool to enhance video analysis. The recorded feedback sessions were conducted three times for each teacher and served as the first source of qualitative data. The feedback sessions were held approximately every three weeks, and each session lasted about 30 minutes. It took almost three months to complete the feedback cycle. Two focus group interview sessions were conducted near the end of the study and served as a second source of qualitative data.

This study combined the Visible Learning educational construct (Hattie, 2009; Fisher et al., 2016) and the Impact Cycle (Knight, 2018). By utilizing the Impact Cycle and Visible Learning, the principal and teachers had a means by which to have meaningful conversations about teaching practices.

The Impact Cycle Checklist (Knight, 2018) was utilized during the feedback sessions to guide the teacher through the improvement process. This checklist assisted the teacher and researcher in making the best decisions about which goals were most appropriate to use for each individual teacher and their students. Consequently, the researcher and participants were able to determine whether particular teaching strategies impacted the quality of instruction.

The feedback cycle between the teachers and principal followed the steps of the Impact Cycle (Knight, 2018): Identify, Learn, Improve. An example of these steps is provided:

1. The teacher and principal collaborated to identify weaknesses in the teacher's instruction after the first video observation and during the first feedback session. They worked together to assess current reality and gained an accurate picture of how to improve instruction effectively and efficiently. The teacher set a goal and selected a strategy to meet that goal.
2. If a teacher asked for assistance, the principal assisted the teacher in learning more about a strategy that could help the teacher to meet their goal. Along the way, additional learning occurred, such as sharing and discussing classroom videos, visiting another teacher's classroom, participating in professional development, reading books or articles, and so forth.
3. During the improvement stage, the teacher reviewed their progress and asked for assistance to confirm direction and invent improvements if needed. This cycle was repeated two more times.

The teachers had complete autonomy in deciding which aspects of their instruction they wanted to video record and share with the principal for the instructional feedback cycle. All of them recorded significantly more instruction than they shared with the principal. This was an added benefit to the process because teachers took additional time to analyze and reflect upon their own instruction.

For the purposes of the feedback sessions, a general rule was to have a 10-to-20-minute video to share and discuss. The feedback sessions were informal and allowed the principal and teacher to talk through the teacher's choices in planning and assessing students' learning. The teachers videoed a variety of lesson types (whole group, small group, direct instruction, etc.) and had flexibility in determining which camera angles would work best and/or which students to video.

BEST PRACTICES FOR IMPLEMENTATION

Because the principal had been at this school for five years, the principal's relationships with the teachers allowed for a natural feedback cycle to occur. The principal focused on building positive working relationships and gaining trust with all teachers and staff so that improvement could occur in a variety of areas.

It was important that the principal understood the unique contexts of the individual participants, as well as the goals and expectations that the participants had for their classroom instruction. A deep understanding of each teacher as an individual is needed for effective feedback and growth to occur. During the research, the interactions seemed to flow freely and authentically, so it seems that this challenge was mitigated.

The feedback sessions were positive and focused on each teacher's strengths and how the principal and teacher could work together to build upon those strengths. If weaknesses were identified, then the teacher and principal collaborated to find a solution to the problem of practice. The teachers found the video analysis treatment to be challenging yet manageable. The principal spent a significant amount of time in classrooms prior to the study to gain a deep understanding of what was happening and how she could best support teachers and students and also provided informal and organic discussions to drive success in all aspects of the school day.

The focus on professional development in the years prior to this study also impacted the success of the research. The teachers and administrators at the school had benefitted from ongoing professional learning sessions during the course of three years that focused on Jim Knight's *Focus on Teaching* (2014a), John Hattie's *Visible Learning* (2009), and Jan Burkins and Kim Yaris's *Who's Doing the Work? How to Say Less so Readers Can Do More* (2016). Additionally, the researcher's vision of a culture of excellence empowered all participants to diligently work toward the common goal of instructional improvement.

TEACHERS' PERCEPTIONS OF VIDEO ANALYSIS AND INSTRUCTIONAL FEEDBACK CYCLE

Upon review of the teachers' perceptions of the feedback cycle's implementation, two overarching themes were illuminated: (1) The use of video analysis positively influenced self-efficacy and collective teacher efficacy by empowering teachers to see a problem of practice, diagnose the problem, and then prescribe an intervention or change in practice; and (2) the element of time spent discussing teaching and learning positively influences instructional effectiveness. While time is a key component of the findings, it is interwoven into the application of the video analysis and feedback process.

The teachers' responses from the feedback sessions and focus group sessions indicated that the treatment of video analysis influenced teachers' self-efficacy. All teachers reported that they felt more confident in their abilities as classroom practitioners because of the video analysis and instructional feedback cycle. While some of the teachers were apprehensive about what they would see in their videos in the beginning of the study, all became more confident with the use of video analysis and in their feedback dialogue by the end of the process.

The feedback sessions with the principal also enabled the teachers to hold focused and deep dialogue about what occurred during the lesson and to focus on goals that would improve their instructional decisions. During the feedback sessions with the principal, the teacher decided on a learning goal, and the principal provided additional support and resources as needed. Knight's forms from *Focus on Teaching* (2014a) were particularly helpful in planning for video collection and analysis. The two most popular forms used during the study were Watch Yourself and Teacher Vs. Student Talk.

The teachers reported that video analysis positively influenced their collective ability to organize and execute courses of action that would produce desired results to impact student learning. This is most likely attributed to the camaraderie that was developed by the group of teachers who participated in the study.

Because this group of teachers had a common goal, they had additional opportunities to discuss problems of practice and how to effectively move forward to achieve their goals. They often discussed their videos with one another, and these extended conversations about their practice created an ongoing sense of collective teacher efficacy and further developed the camaraderie among the participants.

Responses from participants revealed that the element of time spent discussing teaching and learning positively influences instructional effectiveness. The findings showed that feedback, along with the video analysis treatment, had a positive influence on the teachers' instructional effectiveness and their sense of teacher efficacy, both self and collective. This is an important finding to the field of education.

All educators and stakeholders want to increase student learning, and there are myriad techniques and strategies that might work. However, as Hattie (2009, 2012) writes, educators must heed the research and utilize the strategies that work *best*. According to the findings of this study, the use of video analysis and feedback given to teachers is a practice that positively impacts teachers' sense of efficacy and instructional effectiveness. In short, a level of difference was achieved in instructional decision making when video analysis was utilized and was evidenced by teachers' responses in the focus group sessions.

The power of video in the development of self-reflection was another important finding. Qualitative findings showed that the use of video analysis was powerful in helping the participants see what actually occurred in their lessons in comparison to what they remembered. Video does not lie

(Knight, 2014a), and this understanding assisted the study's participants in closely examining what happened instead of what the teachers thought had happened. The rich and detailed conversations about classroom instruction would not have been experienced without the use of video analysis.

The use of video allowed the teacher and administrator to gain a clear picture of reality, and they had meaningful discussions about next steps in instruction. Teachers are likely to become used to what they observe every day, and their understanding of class dynamics often become less accurate over time. The video analysis treatment improved the participants' understanding of their strengths and weaknesses and provoked teacher learning.

The feedback sessions between each participant and the principal were found to be helpful to both parties as they empowered both teacher and principal to see and discuss together the intricacies of teaching and learning. The process promoted teacher agency when teachers decided which element of their instruction they wanted to work on. The participants determined their own learning opportunities, and the feedback from the shared observations provided a powerful influence on teacher learning (Clarke, 2017). Additionally, the reflection process was key to the changes made.

The Visible Learning construct was found to be an important factor in teacher learning. Fisher and colleagues (2016) wrote, to accomplish visible learning, students must understand what they are learning and why they are learning it. They must also understand what success in the learning encompasses. Teachers, too, must hold a deep understanding of what student learning entails and how to achieve it. The concepts of surface, deep, and transfer learning (Fisher et al., 2016) were discussed among the participants and principal many times throughout the study.

When concerns were raised over students who struggled with their learning, often the conversation circled back to whether the students had mastered surface and deep learning in the particular content area and then the reason(s) for the lack of transfer learning was often discovered. Learning intentions and success criteria became a part of the dialogue in the research site since the fall of 2019.

As a result, the Visible Learning philosophy had become part of the fabric of the school and played a significant role in teachers' ongoing dialogue regarding the impact they expected to have on student learning. Hattie's (2009) "hinge point" of 0.40 and his barometer of influence were a determining factor in many of the strategies that the participants chose.

There is a great need for ongoing collaboration between school leaders and teachers so that all can work together to provide effective instruction that positively impacts student learning and achievement. The issues that educators must fix are too large for individuals to accomplish alone. Ongoing collaboration between the participants and the principal was an important factor in instructional improvement, and success most likely would not have been accomplished without it.

The data from this study showed that teacher efficacy was increased from the beginning of the study to the end. This is attributed to a few different factors. Because each individual teacher's self-efficacy increased, a resulting end product was that collective teacher efficacy also increased.

The ongoing collaboration that occurred during the study had positive effects on each teacher, both individually and collectively. This was significant because it suggests that strong instructional leadership is crucial in the facilitation of reinforcing organizational belief systems, which foster student learning. School leadership and teacher collaboration, in harmony with one another, contributed to instructional effectiveness because teacher efficacy was strengthened.

IMPLICATIONS FOR PRACTITIONERS

This study has implications that are relevant to principal practitioners, district and state boards of education, professional development organizations, and teacher preparation programs. The interdependent constructs of teachers' sense of efficacy and instructional effectiveness are important considerations in the field of education and hold a pivotal role in the collective work to improve teaching and learning.

The use of video analysis helped the participants and the principal to collaborate in finding a solution to a problem of practice. For instance, math fact fluency had been an ongoing problem at the school. For years, local testing data indicated that a majority of students struggled with learning math facts with automaticity, flexibility, and fluency. Many discussions about this problem have taken place for years, and numerous professional developments to address the problem had been offered.

Some progress had been made according to various local data points, but there was still a significant number of students who were unable to learn their math facts so that they were successful with math content. This lack of math fact fluency negatively impacts students' future success in math. During the study, two teachers videoed their math instruction, and in both cases, the teachers reported that watching their videos enabled them to understand their students' thinking.

In the busyness of teaching, it is difficult for teachers to notice students' misunderstandings, but when these two teachers watched their own math instruction, they were able to better understand the students' line of thinking. This, in turn, informed their instruction and intervention so that they could more strategically support student learning.

The principal realized that her feedback to teachers needed to be more targeted and individualized. This is difficult to accomplish in any school due the number of teachers and students and the seemingly limitless responsibilities that a school principal has. The dialogue between each individual teacher and the principal during the feedback sessions revealed that every teacher has different strengths and weaknesses, and each teacher has different professional development needs.

The results of the research highlighted the need for the principal to make an ongoing and concerted effort to provide professional development that was targeted to each teacher's needs. This will be difficult to accomplish, but it is an important need that would result in more effective instruction and therefore, improve student learning and achievement.

The key to success is ensuring that teachers have the expertise needed to effectively move forward in their planning, collaboration, instruction, and assessments. Results like this do not happen after a few days of professional development. It takes years of building trusting relationships, planning meaningful professional development, constantly monitoring all manner of data points in all content areas, and always reassessing and changing course when needed. It takes hard work and dedication to teaching and learning.

The National Board process also played a critical role in the success of this study. It should be noted that four of the teachers were going through the National Board process, and because of their National Board candidacy, they have gone through a rigorous process designed to empower them to further their understanding and application of teaching and learning.

CONCLUSION

It is important to note that 100 percent of the teachers in the study reported that their abilities as classroom practitioners were improved through video analysis within an instructional feedback cycle. The use of video analysis increased self-efficacy and collective teacher efficacy because it empowered teachers to see a problem of practice, diagnose the problem, and then prescribe an intervention or change in practice. These findings were significant and provide practitioners with current research that has the potential to impact instructional practices and supervision.

Video analysis can be used as a collaboration tool to increase application of ideas and strategies and can improve teachers' understanding and conversations around what works best in their classrooms. In particular, school administrators should consider the use of video analysis as they have myriad responsibilities and very little time; video analysis offers flexibility and there are fewer time constraints because the administrator can watch the video anytime.

The authors are hopeful that this research can positively impact teachers' instruction and, thereby, student learning and achievement. The importance of teachers' strong sense of efficacy and their instructional effectiveness cannot be underestimated in gaining ground on student learning.

The authors aim to initiate more conversations about what should occur between educators who work in the field and those who support (i.e., district offices and teacher preparation programs) toward achievement of the common goal of improving teaching and learning. The task is difficult but not insurmountable. Finding what works best in relation to teaching and learning is paramount to the future success of America's students.

An effective school leader can be a catalyst for change and can thereby improve both teaching and learning. A simple way to affect true change is to utilize video analysis to improve teachers' sense of efficacy and instructional effectiveness. The use of video analysis enhances teachers' understanding of what actually happens in their classrooms and allows them to adjust when needed. This process is easy to implement and can be very beneficial to both teachers and students.

Twenty-first-century technology provides ease of use to implement video analysis on any given day. Any teacher in any school can utilize video analysis and can experience improvement in a matter of days. Video analysis can be used as a collaboration tool to increase application of new or old ideas and strategies and can improve teachers' understanding and conversations around what works best in their classrooms.

In particular, school leaders should consider the use of video analysis as they have myriad responsibilities and very little time. Plainly stated, video analysis offers flexibility and there are fewer time constraints with video analysis because the administrator can watch the video anytime. School leaders must be catalysts for change because "every student deserves a great teacher, not by chance, but by design" (Fisher et al., 2016, p. 2).

Finding what works best in relation to teaching and learning is paramount to the future success of America's students. It is critical that educators and stakeholders hold a solid understanding of what really happens in classrooms and what needs to be adjusted in order to positively impact student learning. It is our moral imperative to improve so that our students are well-prepared to lead productive and fulfilled lives.

POSTREADING REFLECTIONS/ACTIVITIES

- Consider how you might use video analysis in your setting. How will teachers respond to your request for them to participate in video analysis? (Remember that video analysis should never be forced upon teachers. They should participate voluntarily.)

- Think about your current instructional feedback practices. Are they effective? Do they help teachers improve instruction?
- How might the use of video analysis and an instructional feedback cycle as tools in the teacher evaluation process assist you in both formative and summative evaluation?

REFERENCES

Baecher, L., & McCormack, B. (2014). The impact of video review on supervisory conferencing. *Language and Education, 29*(2), 153–73. https://doi.org/10.1080/09500782.2014.992905

Balyer, A., & Ozcan, K. (2020). School principals' instructional feedback to teachers: Teachers' views. *International Journal of Curriculum and Instruction, 12,* 191–98. https://doi.org/10.3200/TCHS.80.4.191-198

Burkins, J., & Yaris, K. (2016). *Who's doing the work? How to say less so readers can do more.* Stenhouse Publishers.

Fisher, D., Frey, N., & Hattie, J. (2016). *Visible learning for literacy: Implementing the practices that work best to accelerate student learning.* Corwin.

Hattie, J. (2009). *Visible Learning: A synthesis of over 800 meta-analyses relating to student achievement.* Routledge.

Hattie, J. (2012, September). Know thy impact. *Educational Leadership, 70*(1), 18–23.

Hollingsworth, H., & Clarke, D. (2017, August 23). *Video as a tool for focusing teaching self-reflection: Supporting and provoking teacher learning.* https://works.bepress.com/hilary_hollingsworth/34/

Knight, J. (2014a). *Focus on teaching using video for high-impact instruction.* SAGE Publications.

Knight, J. (2014b). What you learn when you see yourself teach. *Educational Leadership, 71*(8), 18–23.

Knight, J. (2018). *The impact cycle what instructional coaches should do to foster powerful improvements in teaching.* SAGE Publications.

Morton, B., & Upton, A. (2020). Collaborative preparation: Educational leaders and school counselors building bridges for effective schools. *The Alabama Journal of Educational Leadership, 7,* 9–17.

National Board for Professional Teaching Standards. (n.d.). *National Board Standards.* https://www.nbpts.org/standards-five-core-propositions

CHAPTER 6

Culturally Responsive Instructional Supervision

(Re)Envisioning Feedback for Equitable Change

Ian M. Mette, Dwayne Ray Cormier, and Yanira Oliveras-Ortiz

PREFOCUS GUIDING QUESTIONS

- How can instructional supervision be used as a tool to address diversity, equity, inclusion, and belonging through ongoing dialogue with teachers?
- What ongoing conversations and scaffolds are needed in school buildings to (re)envision feedback about instruction that has often been ahistorical, apolitical, and context neutral?
- What role should the principal play in developing a team of educators to establish instructional supervision practices and feedback processes that can help create more inclusive and equitable instruction?

INTRODUCTION

Starting in the 1990s, an increasing amount of literature on educational leadership emerged that acknowledged the sociocultural realities of needing to develop inclusive and equitable instruction in the United States. Often described as the sociocultural gap, this work highlighted the vastly different lived experiences and cultural knowledge of many teachers in the United States, many of whom are female and white, and students in the United States who come from historically marginalized backgrounds (Castro, 2010; Cormier, 2020; Gay, 1993).

From this line of research came important developments regarding how US educators might unlearn how they have been socialized to think about privileged identities. Frameworks such as *culturally responsive teaching* (Gay, 1993, 2018), *culturally relevant pedagogy* (Ladson-Billings, 1995, 2017), *culturally responsive school leadership* (Khalifa et al., 2016), and *culturally and historically responsive literacy* (Muhammad, 2020) have all greatly added to the field of education.

These frameworks articulate how educational leaders must attend to identities such as race, class, gender, culture, language, sexual orientation, and identity, among other factors; specifically how identities relate to what is taught, how it is taught, and how what is taught addresses the historical realities of the United States in order to develop more equitable and inclusive outcomes for all students.

Notably missing from these frameworks is the lack of literature related to instructional supervision. Principals in the United States, upward of 80 percent who are white (NCES, 2016), must be willing and able to reflect deeply on their own sociocultural identities in order to help address the instructional inequities that exist in their schools across the country (Cormier & Padney, 2021; Villegas & Lucas, 2002).

Throughout this chapter, we present the idea of culturally responsive instructional supervision (CRIS) to help principals use feedback about observed instruction to support, address, and if needed, confront, instructional practices to improve equitable outcomes for all students in the United States.

As such, the goal of CRIS is not to be "clinical" about how feedback is provided. Rather, the intent of CRIS is to serve as a vehicle for opening a dialogue about history and society—and how teams of educators from representative/diverse backgrounds can work together to support critical reflective stances about how instruction is provided.

Moreover, CRIS can help contribute to (re)envisioning the paradigm about data collected in schools and how it is perceived, specifically to signal a cultural shift in the United States that there is more to education than generating high test scores, a concept that for over twenty years has dominated the failed educational accountability experiment.

Instructional supervision is defined as a formative process, through which a supervisor provides a teacher with supportive feedback with the intent of improving instruction (Mette et al., 2017). There are multiple methodological approaches to instructional supervision that are designed to help educators reflect on teaching practices by collecting observation data to pinpoint feedback on praise, student engagement, and higher order thinking, among other areas of instructional improvement (Zepeda, 2016).

In short, instructional supervision is often viewed as a "missing link" that helps bridge the gap between theory to practice in schools. Often defined as "clinical," it is a practice that implies it is free of subjectivity together with objective feedback on how to best improve instruction.

THE GROWING NEED FOR CULTURALLY RESPONSIVE INSTRUCTIONAL SUPERVISION

Education in the United States in neither objective nor is it free of political ideology (Freire, 1970). Increasingly, there is growing momentum across the United States to prevent discussion about the racialized history of the United States, specifically suppressing the political and moral actions that supported slavery that serve as the bedrock for today's modern racialized society in the United States (Mills, 1997).

Given the definitions and descriptions of instructional supervision, one might envision instructional supervision as the perfect opportunity to use daily observations of instruction to discuss critical and sociocultural perspectives regarding the history of racial and ethnic discrimination in the United States.

Using the cover of objectivity, instructional supervision has allowed for conservative and colorblind ideologies about educational practices in the United States to be perpetuated, failing to consider how positionality, intersectionality, and privilege influence not only how feedback about instruction is given, but also how it is received (Cormier & Padney, 2021).

What results are ideologies about instructional improvement practices that attempt to be apolitical or ahistorical, and as such actively prevent instructional leaders from discussing how identities play an active role in inhibiting the creation of more inclusive and just education systems that produce equitable outcomes for all.

To reestablish itself as a methodology that can help close the theory-practice gap in education, instructional supervision must be reconceptualized to address the sociocultural gap that is perpetuated in US schools. The (re)envisioning of instructional supervision, both in theory and in practice, requires educators to confront the lack of diversity and representation present in how feedback about teaching is provided and perceived.

It also requires practitioners and theorists to stop assuming instructional supervision should be objective or clinical. Instead, educators must acknowledge that if our education system is ever to work toward a more socially just and equitable society, we must reject notions of ahistorical or apolitical beliefs about education.

Given the rapidly diversifying US student population, CRIS can serve as a framework to help produce equity-oriented instructional leaders. Using the foundations put forward by other culturally responsive education theories (Gay, 1993; Khalifa et al., 2016; Muhammad, 2020), CRIS requires instructional leaders to acknowledge that the United States is a modern racialized society as well as one that finds nuanced ways to discriminate about a variety of identities.

Instructional supervision should be seen as a vehicle for having open and honest conversations that are free from political restrictions, specifically those that prevent conversations discussing social disparities (Ford, 1998).

This includes the freedom to provide feedback about instruction that, for many historically marginalized students, represents a system of oppression based on race, ethnicity, gender, and class, among other aspects of identity. Specifically, CRIS requires leaders deeply reflect upon and consider how their identity is a foundational part of how they provide feedback, and how their feedback is received, within the experience of the US education system. The proposed reenvisioning of supervision requires instructional leaders to be willing and able to do the following:

1. acknowledge white supremacy globally and in US society, historically and currently, particularly how this influences what is taught in language arts and social studies curricula;
2. unpack the political and moral actions which supported slavery that are still present in US society today through antiblack sentiment and actions that are reinforced by policies and practices at state and local levels when discussing the racialized history of the United States; and,
3. discuss the widely varied continuum of the lived experiences in modern US society and how these inequities are perpetuated in schools across nondominant sociocultural identities (i.e., confronting anti-immigrant, anti-trans, elitist nationalist ideologies, etc.).

Using this as a foundation for providing feedback about observed teaching, CRIS can be used to provide instructional leaders with a paradigm that centers identity at the core of how educators think about improving outcomes for all students. For example, supervisors need to be able to address instruction that centers whiteness and Eurocentric perspectives when conducting walkthroughs, which allows instructional leaders to focus on instructional inequities based on dominant racial and cultural identities.

Additionally, instructional leaders need to be able to reinforce and celebrate instruction based on observational data that centers less-privileged identities, including lessons that address inequities based on class, gender, orientation, and identity.

Using CRIS as a foundation, instructional leaders can develop methodologies to collect data about teaching that empowers teachers and students to contribute to the creation of a more equitable US society. Perhaps the most powerful aspect of CRIS is for instructional supervisors to develop a more advanced equity lens that asks critical questions such as, "Is whiteness being decentered or recentered in this lesson?"; "What dominant identity (i.e., gender, class, religion, etc.) is this instruction serving?"; and "Is this lesson perpetuating or confronting inequities in US society?"

To achieve this outcome, however, will require groups of educators that represent a wide variety of identities across the United States, not solely principals, to engage in instructional supervision and provide critical formative feedback.

THE IMPORTANCE OF BEING INTENTIONAL WITH REPRESENTATION

Considering 80 percent of all principals in the United States are white, instructional supervision, specifically the endeavor to improve teaching and learning based on formative feedback about observed instruction from one educator to another, should no longer be considered a one-person endeavor. Instead, teams of instructional leaders, not only school administrators, should be created to ensure intentional representation of instructional supervisors that are positioned to provide constructive feedback about inclusive and just instructional practices within schoolhouses.

Based on the racialized history of the United States, when developing the instructional supervision teams, race should be at the center of representation, however other identities such as gender, ethnicity, socioeconomic status, sexual identity, and orientation should also be considered. Through the creation of these teams, schools can provide specific, critical feedback about instructional practices that can be used to challenge hegemonic structures that perpetuate the perceived notion of an education system of oppression in the United States.

Once these teams are established, teacher leaders and administrators should work collectively to determine how and when to provide feedback about observed teaching and learning, as well as what the feedback should be based on. It is of critical importance that teams of educators providing CRIS work in a democratic fashion to develop schoolwide, equity-based supervision goals.

Once these goals are established and approved by the faculty, specific data can be collected and presented back to individual teachers, as well as entire faculty groups to engage in and discuss what the data says about instructional practices within the schoolhouse. Cycles of instructional supervision data can lead to deeper conversations about what is working based on observed instructional methods, what needs to change to lead to more equitable outcomes for students, and how job-embedded individual and schoolwide professional development can lead to more culturally responsive teaching and learning.

One of the most important aspects of instructional supervision is how to provide feedback to a teacher when an observed teaching practice is problematic. When implementing the idea of CRIS, candid feedback is especially important when a member of the intentionally representative supervision team observes an instructional practice that is culturally damaging. One framework to consider is an adaption of the Supervisory Behavior Continuum (Glickman et al., 2017), which can be used to determine how to apply the following:

1. Directive control (the teacher is unaware of culturally damaging instruction, requiring the supervisor to provide explicit feedback and specific opportunities for improvement)
2. Directive informational (the teacher is aware instruction is culturally damaging, requiring the supervisor to provide feedback and a selection of opportunities for improvement)
3. Collaborative (teacher aware their instruction is inclusive; however, the teacher requests candid feedback to actively engage in discussions to reduce marginalization of groups)
4. Nondirective (teacher is seen as a leader in the schoolhouse; they are aware they exist in a system of oppression and are committed to permanently altering the education system)

Based on the transformation of consciousness by the teacher, CRIS can help drive reflection and growth that leads to greater awareness of structural inequities in the United States. As such, the goal of this type of formative feedback, at least initially, should not be used to highlight teacher deficiencies, but rather as a support structure to improve relationships with students and increase equitable outcomes regarding student success.

What results from intentional representation is a supervision team that can help make shifts in instructional practice. Over time, schools can move away from the damaging accountability practices embedded in the US education systems as a result of decades of mandates since the inception of NCLB, and begin to shift towards the responsibility of providing instruction that teaches about and addresses the discriminatory society of the United States.

As such, supervision teams can work together to help challenge the perception of education being seen as a system of oppression, and instead function as a liberatory form of school improvement that helps heal US society.

REFLECTIVE STANCES THAT TRANSLATE TO EQUITABLE OUTCOMES

Developing self-reflective teachers who ponder instructional practices through feedback is an important part of shifting away from accountability and toward social responsibility to help reimagine education in the United States. As with the need to move away from a single principal providing instructional supervision to a representative team, so too is the need to drive ongoing reflection at the personal level. The development of internal culturally responsive reflective stances about instructional practices results in:

1. supportive instructors who remain vigilant about their own self-awareness about teaching;
2. critical colleagues who engaging in peer supervision and provide candid feedback;
3. learning asynchronously about inclusive instructional practice through social media; and,
4. incorporating learning into the local community to celebrate inclusive learning.

To remain vigilant about self-awareness and teaching skills, educators must be committed to continually reflecting on their instruction in a variety of ways. Self-reflective practices include journaling about instruction, analyzing self-collected data about instructional practices and student engagement, and watching self-recorded videos to increase awareness of instruction and teaching practices that might be culturally damaging. Increasingly, teachers can also benefit from quarterly or semester-based student and parent perception surveys about how their instruction and interactions with students and families.

Central to the effort of becoming vigilant about self-awareness must be the teacher's commitment to engage in non-directive development, where a teacher consistently reflects upon how instruction acknowledges the historically marginalized and actively considers the sociocultural gap within the United States.

A second step in increasing responsibility to improve instruction can come through the development of critical colleague groups that offer peer feedback. Feedback provided by peers typically is perceived by teachers as more useful than feedback from a principal (Zepeda, 2016), and this type of instructional supervision supports flattening hierarchical structures that are essential in developing more culturally responsive practices.

These peer groups provide an important additional layer of collective responsibility to support the development of instructional practices that consider various sociocultural perspectives. Additionally, these peer feedback practices can increase the likelihood of vulnerable reflection about race, culture, and the lived experiences of those marginalized in US society and, over time, lead to greater interrogation of teachers' own cultural identities.

In addition to developing critical colleague groups, a third step in developing reflective stances about instruction can come when educators engage in group learning outside of their professional setting. Reducing groupthink and incorporating new ideas from other buildings, particularly what can be learned from other educators through social media, contributes to more democratic thinking about education systems (Glickman & Mette, 2020).

Being intentional about the exchange of ideas is important when engaging in group learning outside of an established professional setting, particularly gaining perspectives that challenge assumptions about dominant ideologies. The result, over time, are groups of educators from diverse cultural backgrounds who are able to engage in CRIS, which leads to equity-minded instruction and student engagement.

A fourth and final step to developing reflective stances about instruction that can lead to more equitable outcomes is establishing a community learning exchange (CLE) process with local stakeholders (Militello et al., 2017). Not only does this allow input from community groups that can be important for educators to hear, but it also provides the opportunity for local stakeholders to share their own stories and voices that are often missing from classrooms.

CRIS seeks to co-construct teaching that honors the cultural experiences of the community it is intended to serve. It does so by assuming responsibility to create inclusive learning experiences for students, as well as parents, that help produce socially just outcomes for all students in the United States.

To help the reader consider practical applications, below are a list of questions both supervisors and teachers should be asking themselves to help translate CRIS into more equitable instruction:

- When analyzing your own instruction or that of others, how do you consider asset-based approaches to instruction rather than deficit-based approaches? How is the instruction you reflect on culturally responsive or democratic and inclusive for all?
- How does the feedback you consider and provide align with the needs of the community that the schoolhouse serves, and is there a clear and observable commitment to social justice?
- In what ways can you suggest incorporating new ideas about the assessment for student learning that considers multiple data sources and that supports student knowledge that is performance based and designed to interact with a community?

While these questions are not exhaustive, they can empower supervisors to prioritize equitable outcomes for students, particularly when reflecting on the learning experience of students who come from historically marginalized groups. These reflections are powerful in that they can occur individually through reflective journaling or through ongoing conversations with teachers.

DEVELOPING DATA COLLECTION TO DRIVE INSTRUCTIONAL IMPROVEMENT

There are a variety of supervision methodologies that can be used to drive dialogue to increase culturally responsive instruction. Different from developing reflective stances about instructional practices—which focuses on intrapersonal and interpersonal dialogue that translate into improved and more equitable outcomes for students—developing culturally responsive instructional supervision methodologies focuses on the collection of data that can be used to grapple with social inequities, critique systemic structures, and challenge dominant cultural perspectives. While not an exhaustive list, these supervision methodologies include the following:

1. Self-study
2. Action research
3. Peer-led observation tools
4. Mini observations collected by an intentionally representative supervision team
5. The Cultural Proficiency Continuum Q-Sort (CPCQ; Cormier, 2020)

Both self-study and action research provide important opportunities to collect data individually or within a small group of trusted peers (Sullivan & Glanz, 2013). This work can include internal reflection or critical reflections with friends about identity, but specifically this focuses on qualitative data to analyze the struggles and successes of becoming more aware of the sociocultural gap in the United States.

Using these data, teachers can develop and reflect upon more equity-minded instructional practices over time. Importantly, these types of methodologies can capitalize on data that lead to change at the individual teacher level and can happen in the absence of support from building level or district-level administrators.

There are also culturally responsive instructional supervision methodologies that require more coordinated efforts. Typically, peer observation structures are based on teams of educators organized by grade level or content area and can contribute to the ongoing development of professional learning communities (Ponicell et al., 2019). Mini observations can be collected to create a dataset across an entire school and provide a mosaic of data points to understand what is happening regarding a specific area of instructional focus, such as student engagement or technology use (Valentine, 2009).

Implementing these as methodological practices requires educators to focus on collecting targeted *observed data points*, such as the implementation of asset-based pedagogies, the presence of investigatory practices that examine racial inequities present in the United States, or the implementation of professional development aimed at closing the sociocultural gap.

On a broader level, there are instructional supervision methodologies that can be used to examine teachers' cultural competence, such as the result of the CPCQ, that can then be used as a quantitative data to provide individualized feedback that can lead to professional development for teachers to better support students who come from historically marginalized backgrounds (Cormier, 2020).

By examining the perceptions of teachers about students who are minoritized, CRIS can individualize supports needed for teachers to increase their cultural competence. Perhaps most important, instructional supervision of this nature avoids congenial aspects of feedback about teaching (Glickman et al., 2017) and instead focuses on teacher-centered supports that lead to social justice.

CONCLUSION: (RE)ENVISIONING INSTRUCTIONAL SUPERVISION TO MESSAGE EQUITY

Developing feedback in schools that incorporates the ideas and practices of culturally responsive instructional supervision signals several important shifts in how feedback about teaching can and should be provided. First and foremost, instructional supervision must shed outdated paradigms about "clinical" and objective feedback, as well as reestablish itself as a critical tool to close the gap between theory and practice so often observed in education.

To accomplish this goal, however, requires the field of supervision, both researchers and practitioners alike, to acknowledge the sociocultural gaps that are present in many schoolhouses across the country and reject apolitical and ahistorical notions of education that fail to recognize the oppressive racialized and discriminatory US society. This requires educators to confront the lack of diversity and representation, how instructional supervision has been provided and perceived up to this point, and to reimagine how feedback about teaching can lead to student learning and engagement that liberates and contributes toward healing in the United States.

To develop a better humanity for all requires principals, the main providers of instructional supervision, to flatten the traditional hierarchical structure of how feedback about instruction has historically been provided. By developing an intentionally representative supervision team, principals and teachers can work together to develop a collective process that is decidedly more democratic.

To make an impact requires educators to acknowledge how the sociocultural gap has persisted throughout the country's history and how US society is steeped in ideologies that supported the enslavement of black people, the colonization of the indigenous nations throughout North America, and the establishment of a crushing capitalist system that produces horrible conditions for those living in poverty.

If the education system is to contribute to bridging sociocultural gaps in the United States, there is also a moral obligation to move away from the accountability structures cemented by the implementation of No Child Left Behind (NCLB). Not only do these structures reinforce whiteness as the norm, but they fail to acknowledge the history of violence, oppression, and cultural dominance perpetuated throughout the United States.

To form coalitions across racial, cultural, and class lines, educators in the United States must not only liberate themselves from whiteness but also contribute to the liberation of historically marginalized groups from the grips of white supremacy. To do so will require instructional leaders to center race and culture, as well as interrogating dominant identities, to challenge hegemonic structures about what instruction is valued in the US education system.

Perhaps most important, implementing culturally responsive instructional supervision will require that school cultures value the deprivatization of teaching. This can be partially accomplished through the creation of intentionally representative instructional supervision teams, particularly in determining when and how to respond to instructional practices that are culturally damaging. Knowing when to apply directive control or directive information supervision is important, particularly if the goal is to transform the consciousness of a teacher to be more collaborative or nondirective in becoming culturally responsive.

The application of CRIS goes beyond keeping classroom doors open—it asks educators to take responsibility for their own instruction, to deeply interrogate their own understanding of what it means to teach to, and to ensure *all students* have equitable outcomes, regardless of their sociocultural background. Through reimagined supervision methodologies, data must be collected and analyzed to develop more equity-minded instructional practices, implement asset-based pedagogies, or pinpoint individualized supports needed for teachers to increase their cultural competence.

There are endless opportunities for culturally responsive instructional supervision—but it can only be a useful theory and practice if instructional leaders understand and value the interconnectedness of every community, our society, and the world more broadly.

POSTREADING REFLECTIONS/ACTIVITIES

- Examine the instructional leadership framework you currently espouse and reflect on your feedback practices. Identify how your positionality

influences how you engage in instructional supervision. What do you notice? How does your social position and power shape your identity as an instructional leader?
- How can educators (re)envision instructional supervision to be more of a collective process, where feedback is used to drive equitable change in the United States that deprivatizes teaching to help create an environment of respect, representation, and reconciliation for the violent and oppressive past in the United States?

REFERENCES

Castro, A. J. (2010). Themes in the research on preservice teachers' views of cultural diversity: Implications for researching millennial preservice teachers. *Educational Researcher, 39*(3), 198–210.

Cormier, D. R. (2020). Assessing preservice teachers' cultural competence with the cultural proficiency continuum q-sort. *Educational Researcher, 50*(1), 17–29. https://doi.org/10.3102/0013189X20936670

Cormier, D. R., & Padney, T. (2021). Semiotic analysis of a foundational textbook used widely across educational supervision. *Journal of Educational Supervision, 4*(2), 101–32.

Freire, P. (1970). *Pedagogy of the oppressed*. Bloomsbury Academic.

Ford, D. Y. (1998). The underrepresentation of minority students in gifted education: Problems and promises in recruitment and retention. *The Journal of Special Education, 32*(1), 4–14.

Gay, G. (1993). Building cultural bridges: A bold proposal for teacher education. *Education and Urban Society*, 285–99.

Gay, G. (2018). *Culturally responsive teaching: Theory, research, and practice* (3rd ed.). Teachers College Press.

Glanz, J. (2021). Personal reflections on supervision as instructional leadership: From whence it came and to where shall it go? *Journal of Educational Supervision, 4*(3), 66–81. https://doi.org/10.31045/jes.4.3.5

Glickman, C. D., Gordon, S. P., & Ross-Gordon, J. M. (2017). *Supervision and instructional leadership: A developmental approach* (10th ed.). Pearson.

Glickman, C., & Mette, I. M. (2020). *The essential renewal of America's schools: A leadership guide to democratizing schools from the inside-out*. Teachers College Press.

Khalifa, M. A., Gooden, M. A., & Davis, J. E. (2016). Culturally responsive school leadership: A synthesis of the literature. *Review of Educational Research, 86*(4), 1272–311. https://doi.org/10.3102/0034654316630383

Ladson-Billings, G. (1995). Toward a theory of culturally relevant pedagogy. *American Educational Research Journal, 32*(3), 465–91. https://doi.org/10.3102/00028312032003465

Ladson-Billings, G. (2017). The (r)evolution will not be standardized. In D. Paris & H. S. Alim (Eds.), *Culturally sustaining pedagogies: Teaching and learning for justice in a changing world* (pp. 141–156). Teachers College Press.

Mette, I. M., Range, B. G., Anderson, J., Hvidston, D. J., Nieuwenhuizen, L., & Doty, J. (2017). The wicked problem of the intersection between supervision and evaluation. *International Electronic Journal of Elementary Education, 9*(3), 709–24.

Militello, M., Ringler, M. C., Hodgkins, L., & Hester, D. M. (2017). I am, I am becoming: How community engagement changed out learning, teaching, and leadership. *International Journal of Qualitative Studies in Education, 30*(1), 58–73.

Mills, C. W. (1997). *The racial contract.* Cornell University.

Muhammad, G. (2020). *Cultivating genius: An equity framework for culturally and historically responsive literacy.* Scholastic.

NCES. (2016). Characteristics of public school teachers. https://nces.ed.gov/programs/coe/indicator_clr.asp

Ponticell, J. A., Zepeda, S. J., Jimenez, A. M., Lanoue, P. D., Haines, J. G., & Ata, A. (2019). Observation, feedback, and reflection. In S. J. Zepeda & J. A. Ponticell (Eds.), *The Wiley handbook of educational supervision* (pp. 251–80). Wiley Blackwell.

Sullivan, S., & Glanz, J. (2013). *Supervision that improves teaching and learning* (4th ed.). Corwin.

Valentine, J. (2009). *The instructional practices inventory: Using a student learning assessment to foster organizational learning.* National Staff Development Council, Annual Convention, St. Louis, MO.

Villegas, A. M., & Lucas, T. (2002). Preparing culturally responsive teachers: Rethinking the curriculum. *Journal of Teacher Education, 53*(1), 20–32.

Welsh, R. O., & Swain, W. A. (2020). (Re)defining urban education: A conceptual review and empirical exploration of the definition of urban education. *Educational Researcher, 49*(2), 90–100.

Zepeda, S. J. (2016). *Instructional supervision: Applying tools and concepts* (4th ed.). Routledge.

CHAPTER 7

Feedback to Improve Culturally Responsive Instruction

Maika Yeigh

PREFOCUS GUIDING QUESTIONS

- How can supervisors identify culturally responsive instructional pedagogies in K–12 classrooms?
- How can supervisors tailor feedback to the context of the learners in the classroom?
- In what ways can reflective thinking and probing questions support a classroom that meets the needs of traditionally marginalized students?

This chapter will provide a brief overview of culturally responsive pedagogy and explain why it should be broadly utilized in K–12 classrooms. The heart of the chapter will focus on a framework that supervisors can use to identify cultural responsiveness during observations. In addition to the markers of culturally responsive instruction for which a supervisor can use during a classroom observation, other tools will be provided, such as specific "look-fors" for each marker, reflective prompts for teachers, and sample probing questions to guide reflection on instructional practices that meet the needs of all students.

INTRODUCTION

With classrooms in the United States increasingly comprised of students from culturally and linguistically diverse backgrounds and the goal to provide every K–12 student with a robust antiracist education, it is critical that teachers understand and implement culturally responsive and sustaining pedagogies to support student learning. Specifically, traditionally marginalized and minoritized students need teachers who build from culturally relevant teaching (Ladson-Billings, 2014), culturally responsive approaches (Gay, 2000), and with a focus on culturally sustaining pedagogies (Paris & Alim, 2014).

It is more critical than ever before for teachers to view students' cultural and linguistic backgrounds, home and community knowledge, and various ways of knowing through an asset-framed lens (López, 2017; Yosso, 2005). Teachers who use culturally responsive teaching pedagogies connect their students lived experiences (i.e., culture, languages, and life experience) with what students are learning in school. When a teacher is responsive to their needs, traditionally marginalized students engage with the curriculum (Abacioglu et al., 2020).

In addition, students with teachers who use culturally responsive instruction build a stronger sense of identity (Linan-Thompson et al., 2018) and engage more deeply with the content in the classroom (Hill, 2012; Lalas & Strikwerda, 2020).

Feeling valued and being engaged are important ingredients for learning. Not surprisingly, then, traditionally marginalized students whose teachers use culturally responsive teaching approaches in their classrooms demonstrate higher achievement levels in contrast to students whose teachers use strategies that are incongruous with students' home and school cultures (Griner & Stewart, 2013; NYSED, 2019). While supporting the use of culturally responsive pedagogies is critical for student success, enactment of strategies to support traditionally marginalized students is more complex.

Many teachers in American classrooms are white, while students of color make up the majority of the school-age population in the United States. According to the National Center for Education Statistics (2021), during the 2017–2018 academic year, 79 percent of public-school teachers were white while over half of the students in public school classrooms identified as students of color.

Even while increasingly serving diverse students, the dominance of Euro-centric culture is ever-present in schools (McGee & Stovall, 2015; Yeigh, 2022). Examples of the influence of Euro-centric culture can be found in many places, including curriculum choices that place the history of black and indigenous cultures into elective courses or focus on texts written by white authors; language hierarchies that discourage the use of home language and cultural dialects in schools; and punitive disciplinary practices that push black children out of classrooms at higher rates than their white classmates.

That said, it is possible for white teachers to build a stance toward culturally responsive teaching with a repertoire of strategies to meet the needs of all learners, including emergent bilingual students and students who come from traditionally marginalized backgrounds. Supervisors play a critical role in supporting teacher growth and development in this area.

SUPERVISORS' ROLE IN ENACTING CULTURALLY RESPONSIVE CLASSROOM PRACTICES

There is much work that supervisors do to support teachers in understanding and implementing culturally responsive pedagogies. Support includes professional development focused on creating classrooms with welcoming and affirming environments, structuring professional learning communities to look at data and hold high expectations for all learners, and designing inclusive curriculum and equitable assessments. Specifically,

> Supervisors are well-positioned to support teachers in developing just and equitable instructional practices. With extensive time in classrooms and close relationships with teachers, supervisors have a window into teachers' everyday interactions with students and the extent to which pedagogy is responsive to students' varying needs and cultural backgrounds. (Garver & Maloney, 2020, p. 330)

However, two persistent and prevalent challenges supervisors face when supporting teacher development in this area include (1) identifying markers of culturally responsive instruction in the classroom, and (2) providing specific and actionable feedback to teachers. Initially, supervisors must understand how educational inequities are revealed in classrooms and how to support teachers in the creation of equitable classrooms (Jacobs, 2014).

MARKERS OF CULTURALLY RESPONSIVE CLASSROOMS

To understand how equitable classrooms can be developed, it is useful to identify distinguishing characteristics of culturally responsive pedagogy. Table 7.1 includes descriptors of culturally responsive instruction to guide

Table 7.1. Markers of a culturally responsive classroom

The teacher:
Exhibits cultural awareness and responsiveness
Demonstrates high expectations and responsibility
Prepares students for rigor and independent learning
Fosters growth mindset in all students
Provides curriculum that is relevant and empowering
Designs assessments that encourage reflective growth
Fosters a variety of student perspectives
Actively encourages students to be change agents
Learning environment affirms and values each child's cultural identities

As seen in students:
Students take ownership of learning
Students respect themselves and their classmates
Students work together to produce learning
Students build relationships with their classmates

supervisors' classroom observations. While the list is not intended to be comprehensive, it is a useful starting point for supervisors to note whether best practices for meeting the needs of culturally and linguistically diverse students are present or whether there are individual and structural factors that continue to perpetuate inequities in classrooms (Jacobs, 2014).

The table is divided into two sections, one for what a supervisor can observe in teacher actions and the other qualities that would be evidenced in observations of the students in the classrooms. If a supervisor is focused on increasing culturally responsive practices in their school context, this list can guide the focus during an observation.

HOW TO LOOK FOR CULTURALLY RESPONSIVE PRACTICES

The descriptors for each marker are broad and can be difficult for teachers to operationalize in the classroom. For supervisors, the descriptors can also be challenging to discern through observation, making it arduous to provide specific and actionable feedback. Breaking down a broad category such as "Fosters growth mindset in all students" into more specific look-fors allows a supervisor to identify the presence of the construct, as well as provide refined feedback. Table 7.2 provides an example of observable information to which a supervisor can reference as they provide feedback to teachers.

The look-fors provided are samples; each construct could have a longer list generated by the supervision team and in concert with the school initiatives and goals.

Look-fors provide specificity, which can be used to create actionable and useful feedback. Sharing with a teacher the suggestion that they can improve on "fostering growth mindset" could be too vague and may not get the desired outcome. Instead, encouraging a teacher to allow students to use home language as a learning support is both unambiguous and specific enough to implement in the classroom. When feedback is clear and focused it is more attainable; specific feedback is easier to implement (Fisher & Frey, 2012).

Table 7.2. Sample construct and accompanying look-fors

Construct	Look-Fors
Fosters growth mindset in all students	• Students actively work to make meaning, regardless of whether they have it "correct." • Students demonstrate critical thinking. • Students are encouraged to "try again." • Students are encouraged to use invented spelling, home language, visual models, and other tools to support learning.

REFLECTIVE PROMPTS

Providing feedback on constructs of culturally responsive teaching is important to move the lever of change in classroom spaces. Among high-leverage feedback strategies, fostering reflective thinking is one of the most effective (Burns et al., 2019), including promoting teacher reflection on the impact of instructional actions within the sociocultural context of classroom spaces (Haberlin, 2019; Price-Dennis & Colmenares, 2021). Teaching is complex; providing specific prompts to guide thinking and conversation can scaffold a teacher toward reflection on culturally responsive practices.

As part of the observation and feedback cycle, supervisor implementation of reflective prompts, either prior to or postobservation, is an important step to bridging the gap between current practice and the target practices the supervisor wants to see during an observation. Table 7.3 has sample prompts to guide reflective thinking on specific aspects of culturally responsive instructional practices.

Like the look-fors, the reflective prompts provided in the table are just a sample; individual teacher goals and school initiatives can drive additional prompted questions for both pre- and postobservation.

Supervisors can use the prompts as part of their preobservation work by asking the teacher to analyze the upcoming learning segment and think through the aspects of culturally responsive teaching on which to focus. For example, when considering the reflective prompt, "How will you/did you build on the different ways of knowing and cultural capital your students bring?" the teacher must actively acknowledge all of the learners in the classroom space, including those whose first language is not English.

When teachers engage with reflective prompts, they can preemptively analyze their lesson plans and think through how they are meeting the needs of their learners by providing culturally responsive practices. Offering a scaffold

Table 7.3. Sample construct, accompanying look-fors, and reflective prompts

Construct	Look-Fors	Reflective prompts
Fosters growth mindset in all students	• Students actively work to make meaning, regardless of whether they have it "correct." • Students demonstrate critical thinking. • Students are encouraged to "try again." • Students are encouraged to use invented spelling, home language, visual models, and other tools to support learning.	• How do you make sure students are comfortable attempting new skills and grappling with the concepts? • How do you model a growth mindset for your students? • In which part of today's lesson will students/did students take academic risks? • How will you/did you build on the different ways of knowing and cultural capital your students bring?

that nudges the teacher toward a metacognitive stance and deeper understanding of culturally responsive methods helps teachers "see" the smaller parts of what some might consider a daunting task (i.e., providing culturally responsive teaching) in manageable chunks that are more easily tackled.

The most difficult—and important—aspect of providing feedback is making sure it is easy for the recipient to understand and easy for the recipient to envision what a change could look like in their classroom. Without this visualization, the steps can seem unattainable. Of course, when people think a goal is out of reach, they are less inclined to make any attempts.

Adding specific steps allows the teacher to break down the goal into smaller steps. The *actions* that occur because of the feedback are how thinking and practices change. To that end, feedback should be specific enough to be *actionable*, thus avoiding the gap that occurs between what the supervisor intended with the actions of the teacher.

PROBING QUESTIONS TO GUIDE ACTIONABLE FEEDBACK

Probing questions are useful to engage a teacher in deeper and reflective thinking and are a mechanism to focus the conversation on specific areas for growth. Probing questions can guide a teacher to an analysis of whether they are using responsive teaching practices. Supervisors can combine reflective feedback and problem solving with actionable steps. Table 7.4 includes probing questions a supervisor can post in order to focus action steps toward fostering growth mindset in all students.

A more comprehensive list of descriptors of culturally responsive instruction, accompanying look-fors, reflective questions, and probing questions to guide supervisors in the observation cycle and provide a useful mechanism to create actionable feedback is located at the end of this chapter (see appendix 7.1).

CONCLUSION

It is urgent to create classroom spaces that support the learning of traditionally marginalized students. As K–12 classrooms in the United States continue to become more diverse, pedagogical approaches must account for the learners in the classrooms and actively work to meet the needs of all students.

Although there are other important steps needed in educational contexts (i.e., diversifying the teaching force, increasing funding to traditionally underserved schools) one mechanism available within the current funding

Table 7.4. Actionable feedback for culturally responsive teaching practices: One sample

Construct	Look-Fors	Reflective Prompts	Probing Questions to Guide Actionable Feedback
Fosters growth mindset in all students	• Students actively work to make meaning, regardless of whether they have it "correct." • Students demonstrate critical thinking. • Students are encouraged to "try again." • Students are encouraged to use invented spelling, home language, visual models, and other tools to support learning.	• How do you make sure students are comfortable attempting new skills and grappling with the concepts? • How do you model a growth mindset for your students? • In which part of today's lesson will students/did students take academic risks? • How will you/did you build on the different ways of knowing and cultural capital your students bring?	• Why do you think students were willing to take risks in this lesson? • What words will you say to a student who is reluctant to fail a task or does not have a skill solidly in place?

models is supervision of classroom teachers. There are many observation protocols in use, but without a focus on both culturally responsive classroom practices as well as providing actionable feedback tied to teacher reflection as a mechanism for concrete improvements, challenges to changing pedagogy will persist.

POSTREADING REFLECTIONS/ACTIVITIES

- Compare the goals in your school improvement plan (SIP) with the constructs for culturally responsive classroom instruction. What adjustments can you make to your SIP to encourage improvement in culturally responsive classroom instructional practices?
- Use Appendix 7.1 to create actionable feedback statements that are specific to your school context and the teachers in your building.
- Practice using Appendix 7.1 with your administrative team using either a teaching video or a mock postobservation debrief.

REFERENCES

Abacioglu, C. S., Volman, M., & Fischer, A. H. (2020). Teachers' multicultural attitudes and perspective taking abilities as factors in culturally responsive teaching. *British Journal of Educational Psychology, 90*(3), 736–52.

Burns, R. W., Jacobs, J., & Yendol-Hopppey, D. (2019). A framework for naming the scope and nature of teacher candidate supervision in clinically-based teacher preparation: Tasks, high-leverage practices, and pedagogical routines of practice. *The Teacher Educator, 55*(2), 214–38. doi.org/10.1080/08878730.2019.1682091

Fisher, D., & Frey, N. (2012). Making time for feedback. *Educational Leadership, 70*(1), 42–46.

Garver, R., & Maloney, T. (2020). Redefining supervision: A joint inquiry into preparing school-based leaders to supervise for equity. *Journal of Research on Leadership Education, 15*(4), 330–55.

Gay, G. (2000). *Culturally responsive teaching: Theory, research, and practice.* Teachers College Press.

Griner, A. C., & Stewart, M. L. (2013). Addressing the achievement gap and disproportionality through the use of culturally responsive teaching practices. *Urban Education, 48*(4), 585–621.

Haberlin, S. (2019). Something always works: A self-study of strengths-based coaching in supervision. *Journal of Educational Supervision, 2*(1), 38–57.

Hattie, J., & Timperley, H. (2007). The power of feedback. *Review of Educational Research, 77*(1), 81–112.

Hill, A. L. (2012). Culturally responsive teaching: An investigation of effective practices for African American learners.

Jacobs, J. (2014). Fostering equitable school contexts: Bringing a social justice lens to field supervision. *Florida Association of Teacher Educators Journal, 1*(14), 1–16.

Ladson-Billings, G. (2014). Culturally relevant pedagogy 2.0: A.k.a. the remix.*Harvard Educational Review, 84*, 74–84.

Lalas, J. W., & Strikwerda, H. L. (2020). Driving equity in action through a socially and culturally situated pedagogy: Culturally relevant teaching and learning as a form of equity toward student engagement. In *Overcoming current challenges in the P–12 teaching profession* (pp. 291–315). IGI Global.

Linan-Thompson, S., Lara-Martinez, J. A., & Cavazos, L. O. (2018). Exploring the intersection of evidence-based practices and culturally and linguistically responsive practices. *Intervention in School and Clinic, 54*(1), 6–13.

López, F. A. (2017). Altering the trajectory of the self-fulfilling prophecy: Asset-based pedagogy and classroom dynamics. *Journal of Teacher Education, 68*(2), 193–212.

McGee, E. O., & Stovall, D. (2015). Reimagining critical race theory in education: Mental health, healing, and the pathway to liberatory praxis. *Educational Theory, 65*(5), 491–511.

National Center for Education Statistics. (2021). Racial/ethnic enrollment in public schools. *Condition of Education.* U.S. Department of Education, Institute of Education Sciences. Retrieved from https://nces.ed.gov/programs/coe/indicator/cge.

New York State Education Department. (2019). Culturally responsive-sustaining education framework. https://www.nysed.gov/crs/framework

Paris, D., & Alim, H. S. (2014). What are we seeking to sustain through culturally sustaining pedagogy? A loving critique forward. *Harvard Educational Review, 84*(1), 85–100.

Price-Dennis, D., & Colmenares, E. (2021). Exploring the impact of field-based supervision practices in teaching for social justice. *Journal of Educational Supervision, 4*(2), 1–22.

Yeigh, M. (2022). White language supremacy: Clarifying the CCCC Position Statement. *The Oregon English Journal, 43*(2).

Yosso, T. J. (2005). Whose culture has capital? A critical race theory discussion of community cultural wealth. *Race, Ethnicity and Education, 8*(1), 69–91.

APPENDIX 7.1

Markers of a Culturally Responsive Classroom to Support Actionable Feedback

Table 7.5.

Construct	Look-Fors	Reflective Prompts	Probing Questions to Guide Actionable Feedback
Exhibits cultural awareness and responsiveness	• In conversations, educator is reflective, open, and honest about their own personal growth toward understanding identity and how it shapes their classroom practices. • Routinely seeks support, resources, and ideas to build on their current understanding of identity, cultural awareness, and biases.	• What work have you done to identify how your own identity, cultural lens, and biases show up in your work? • Tell me about the identities of the students in your classroom. • Which languages are spoken by your students and their families? When can students use their home language in the classroom?	• What next steps will you take? • What have you learned so far about your students? What else would you like to learn?
Demonstrates high expectations and responsibility	• Classroom interactions demonstrate the belief that all students can and will learn. • Restorative practices are used by all classroom stakeholders; students hold themselves and each other accountable for learning using language of kindness.	• What strategies are you using to encourage and communicate high expectations for all learners? • How do you make sure all students, including students learning English, understand your expectations?	• Do each of your students know that you have high expectations for them? How do you know? If not, who do you need to spend more time building up and how might you do it?

Construct	Look-Fors	Reflective Prompts	Probing Questions to Guide Actionable Feedback
Prepares students for rigor, independent, and collaborative learning	• The work provided is meaningful. • Students take on most of the cognitive load. • The lesson has a balance between teacher led and collaborative or independent practice.	• How do you turn thinking over to your students? • How do students understand themselves as learners and contributing members of the classroom? • What scaffolds do you have in place for students who are learning English?	• Which part of this lesson required students to think hard and do challenging work? • How do you make sure all students can access today's content? What additional supports might students learning English need?
Fosters growth mindset in all students	• Students actively work to make meaning, regardless of whether they have it "correct." • Students demonstrate critical thinking. • Students are encouraged to "try again." • Students are encouraged to use invented spelling, home language, visual models, and other tools to support learning.	• How do you make sure students are comfortable attempting new skills and grappling with the concepts? • How do you model a growth mindset for your students? • In which part of today's lesson will students/ did students take academic risks? • How will you/did you build on the different ways of knowing and cultural capital your students bring?	• Why do you think students were willing to take risks in this lesson? • What words will you say to a student who is reluctant to fail a task or does not have a skill solidly in place?

(continued)

Table 7.5. *Continued*

Construct	Look-Fors	Reflective Prompts	Probing Questions to Guide Actionable Feedback
Provides curriculum that is relevant and empowering	• Curriculum (i.e., materials, activities, structures) provide opportunities for multiple and non-dominant perspectives to be shared/explored; the question "whose voice is missing?" is asked or alluded to.	• How do you decide on curriculum that is important to the community?	• Whose perspectives were shared in today's lesson? Whose perspective was missing? • What additional materials or perspectives can you bring in for your next lesson?
Designs assessments that encourage reflective growth	• Timely and actionable feedback is provided to students. • Students are expected to redo assignments to demonstrate growth. • Grades reflect growth and achievement, not where they started. • Grades focus on student learning, not behaviors.	• Do students know what they are expected to know and be able to do? • How do your assessments reaffirm a growth mindset? • What feedback can be provided so students understand their next steps?	• How does today's assessment encourage students to try again if they do not get it the first time? • How can students who are learning English demonstrate learning on today's assessment?
Fosters a variety of student perspectives	• A variety of perspectives are shared in class.	• How do you help students respond to each other respectfully? • How do you encourage the sharing of different perspectives in your classrooms, including those with which you might disagree?	• What techniques might you use to support the sharing of ideas? • What contrasting ideas or perspectives might you anticipate in today's lesson?

Construct	Look-Fors	Reflective Prompts	Probing Questions to Guide Actionable Feedback
Actively encourages students to be change agents	• Language of empowerment (i.e., I can, I will, I intend to) is used in the classroom. • Change agents from a variety of cultural contexts are explored.	• How do your lessons empower students to act as agents for social change? • How do your lessons draw parallels between issues important to your students and their agency as humans?	• Where do the issues your students care about appear in your classroom? • How can students get involved in the issues that matter to them?
Learning environment affirms and values each child's cultural identities	• Students bring any/all aspects of their cultural identities into the classroom (i.e., use home language, cultural dress, family structure).	• How do you affirm and value the various aspects of students' cultural identities?	• Which students might more readily share their cultural identities in class? • How might individual identities "appear" in the work that students produce?
Students take ownership of learning	• There is time in class for students to reflect on their learning and set goals for next steps. • Evidence of goal setting is prevalent within the classroom (i.e., reflective prompts on walls, language of "drafts").	• When do you provide time for students to set goals for their own learning? • Can you build in more time for students to take ownership of their progress toward meeting their goals?	• What sort of impact do you think it has on students when they reflect on what they know so far?

(continued)

Table 7.5. *Continued*

Construct	Look-Fors	Reflective Prompts	Probing Questions to Guide Actionable Feedback
Students respect themselves and their classmates	• Students use classroom resources and take care of their needs (i.e., materials, restroom access). • Students' actions support the learning environment for their classmates. • Restorative practices are used by all classroom stakeholders; people use caring language with one another.	• How do your classroom expectations encourage students to take care of/responsibility for their personal and learning needs? • In what ways do your students' culture shape the way they interact in the classroom? • Which routines are working well in your classroom?	• Why do you think the routines are working well during the opening part of class? • What routines would you want to change in other parts of the class?
Students work together to produce learning	• Students all have a role in cooperative learning activities. • All students participate in the group. • Conflicts are resolved through active listening and communication.	• How do you design collaborative tasks to ensure positive interdependence and equal participation of all members? • How do you help students communicate their needs and understand those of their peers during group work? • How do you support quieter or traditionally marginalized voices in the group?	• Which group was most successful in today's lesson? • Which group could use additional supports? • What supports can you provide for students learning English? • How can you help a quieter student get more involved in the group?

Construct	Look-Fors	Reflective Prompts	Probing Questions to Guide Actionable Feedback
Students build relationships with their classmates	• Students sit and work with many classmates. Students know each other's names and use them in the classroom context. • There are no "outliers" in the classroom.	• How do you help students get to know one another? • How do you help students build relationships with one another? • How do you "bring in" students who might feel excluded or who are learning English?	• Who might have been left out of today's lesson? • What sort of impact do you think it has on the classroom environment when students know one another?

SECTION II

Specific Applications of Feedback

CHAPTER 8

Building Leadership Content Knowledge to Supervise Teachers in STEM Disciplines

Sarah Quebec Fuentes, Jo Beth Jimerson, and Mark A. Bloom

PREFOCUS GUIDING QUESTIONS

- What were your experiences as a student or teacher in science and mathematics classes? How do those experiences affect you when observing STEM classes?
- What kinds of feedback do you offer that you consider "content-neutral"?
- In what content area(s) are you most confident in your knowledge and ability to provide actionable feedback to teachers? What are your strengths and challenges in working with teachers in STEM fields?

INTRODUCTION

School leaders already face challenges of time, logistics, and engagement in difficult and candid conversations with teachers as they work to provide actionable feedback. These challenges can be daunting when school leaders work with teachers outside their area of teaching expertise, including science, technology, engineering, and mathematics (STEM) fields (Quebec Fuentes & Jimerson, 2020). School leaders not well-versed in STEM-specific content or teaching approaches may experience limited effectiveness in efforts to provide teachers with relevant, credible, and actionable feedback.

Supporting teacher growth and development is a primary responsibility of school leaders (Hitt & Tucker, 2016), but this is easier said than done when leaders must work across gaps in familiarity with content and content-specific pedagogy (i.e., pedagogical content knowledge). No school leader can know everything about every content area. At the same time, a basic level of knowledge provides a useful lens to help leaders understand what they see and hear in classrooms. As their understanding affects the kinds of feedback they provide, disciplinary knowledge can help leaders provide more actionable feedback to teachers.

Leaders can equip themselves to bridge gaps to support teacher development by building *leadership content knowledge* (LCK), which is "knowledge of academic subjects that is used by administrators when they function as instructional leaders" (Stein & Nelson, 2003, p. 423). Gradual development of LCK provides a way for leaders to build familiarity with content and content-specific pedagogy to engage with teachers in informed and credible ways.

This chapter describes LCK's role in enabling actionable feedback to teachers in STEM fields, steps school leaders can take to build STEM LCK, and existing district structures that support school leaders' development of STEM LCK.

CHALLENGES TO ACTIONABLE FEEDBACK IN STEM

School leaders are a critical but largely *indirect* influence on student learning; that is, school leaders typically support improvements in student learning to the degree they recruit, hire, and support effective teachers. Whether supporting an early career or experienced teacher, a main pathway to teacher growth is the process of supervision and evaluation, which can include learning walks, quick classroom observations, or the use of more formal rubrics and checklists. While evaluation is understood to be a final, or at least very formal judgment on aspects of a teacher's work, supervision is supposed to be an ongoing process aimed at improvement.

Supervision requires trust between supervisor and supervisee—the supervisee has to feel safe in making mistakes and acknowledging professional needs. In contrast, evaluation procedures can challenge the establishment of trust, as teachers may fear that if they admit mistakes or knowledge gaps, their employment will be at risk. This challenge can be magnified when teachers encounter supervisors who lack expertise in STEM, thus limiting their ability to provide credible and actionable feedback (Lochmiller, 2016).

Actionable feedback, communicated to a teacher by a supervisor, spurs reflection about or guides teacher practice for structuring and facilitating student learning in a classroom. Actionable feedback may take the form of a specific suggestion or of data that help a teacher better understand a problem of practice they are investigating. Such feedback must be timely, concrete, connected to the immediate work of the teacher, and result in a clear understanding of what can or should be changed in the classroom context and how it can be changed.

When teachers have sufficient knowledge and experience to identify gaps between intended and actual performance, leaders may function as a critical friend or thinking partner (Glickman et al., 2017). On the other hand, teachers may lack the knowledge or experience needed to identify gaps that are getting in the way of student learning. In these cases, the school leader may need to take a more directive role in identifying such areas and connecting the teacher to resources or other professional learning to address the gaps (Glickman et al., 2017).

Unfortunately, not all school leaders are well-equipped to provide the kinds of feedback needed to help teachers in STEM disciplines grow (Lochmiller & Acker-Hocevar, 2016). Providing useful feedback requires a constellation of skills, including the following:

- Self-awareness of knowledge or lack thereof relative to the content area being supervised
- Communication and relationship-building skills
- Knowledge of a range of content-neutral practices that increase student learning
- Understanding of content-specific curricular targets (standards) across grade levels
- A degree of familiarity with how core content-related practices are taught and assessed

Ignoring these factors hinders the provision of credible, concrete, and content-sensitive feedback.

Without a base level of understanding about what characterizes high-quality instruction in STEM disciplines, some leaders may avoid providing feedback (Lochmiller, 2016; Lochmiller & Acker-Hocevar, 2016). Other leaders may resort to hyperfocusing on content-neutral practices (e.g., formative assessment, differentiation, general questioning strategies) or atmospheric elements of the classroom, such as feel, organization, and student engagement (Quebec Fuentes & Jimerson, 2020). When these facets constitute the majority of leader-teacher talk around instruction, such feedback may do little to improve STEM instruction.

DEVELOPING LCK IN STEM VIA POSTHOLING

Although no leader can know *everything*, all leaders can step into the role of lead learner (Fullan, 2016). Leaders who want to be well-equipped to provide actionable feedback commit to learning about field-specific core concepts, common misconceptions, and discipline-sensitive instructional strategies (Cunningham & Lochmiller, 2020; Quebec Fuentes & Jimerson, 2020). One strategy leaders can use to build knowledge in STEM is to engage in *postholing*.

Originally described by Stein and Nelson (2003), postholing provides a helpful way of thinking about the process of developing LCK. For those unfamiliar with how fences are often constructed in farm and ranch territory, one of the first steps is to dig holes sufficiently deep—but not terribly wide—to anchor fenceposts. Leaders who posthole engage in

> In-depth explorations of an important but bounded slice of the subject, how it is learned, and how it is taught. The purpose of postholing is to learn how knowledge is built in that subject, what learning tasks should look like, and what good instruction looks like. (Stein & Nelson, 2003, p. 446)

School leaders who adopt a postholing approach develop STEM LCK through individually driven practices and by taking advantage of existing district structures.

As individuals, leaders engage in a targeted process to deepen STEM-specific knowledge (Quebec Fuentes & Jimerson, 2019). The process, the LCK Challenge, starts with identifying a content area to focus learning over one school year. The leader asks a content-area expert (e.g., instructional coach) to share organizations that offer publications, conferences, and resources that support learning of discipline-specific, research-based practices. With expert support, the leader sets out learning goals and makes a four-pronged plan aligned to these goals (figure 8.1). Leaders share their intentions with faculty, incorporate reflection, and report on their progress.

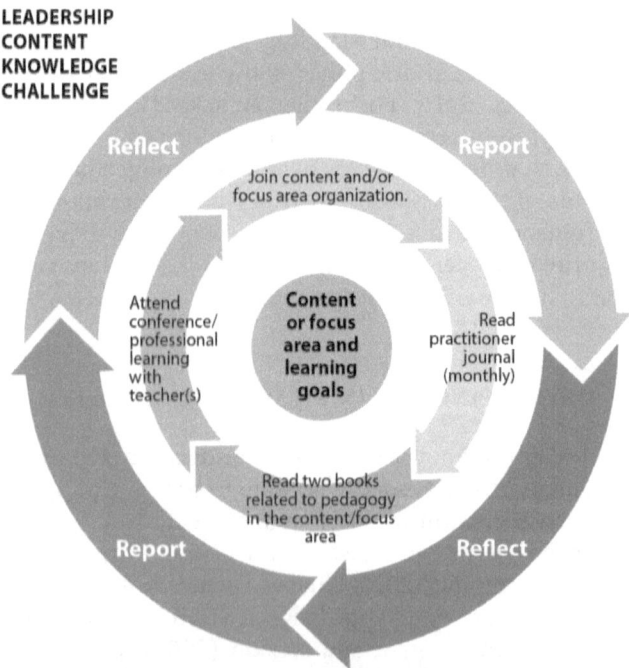

Figure 8.1. Leadership content knowledge challenge
Source: Quebec Fuentes & Jimerson, 2019, p. 33; Used with permission of Learning Forward, www.learningforward.org. All rights reserved.

Some districts have learning opportunities purposefully designed for school leaders to develop their LCK; however, these are uncommon. Fortuitously, school districts have existing structures that can be repurposed for leaders to build their LCK. In concert with existing structures (e.g., Ford et al., 2020; Jimerson & Quebec Fuentes, 2021a, 2021b), leaders working to build knowledge related to STEM instruction can do the following:

- Engage in learning walks with expert teachers and instructional specialists
- Attend content-focused professional learning targeted for teachers
- Integrate LCK-building activities into existing Professional Learning Networks
- Use artifacts (e.g., observation and evaluation rubrics) as springboards for discussion

By engaging in the LCK Challenge and reframing existing district structures, school leaders make a commitment to building LCK in their development as an instructional leader.

EXAMPLES OF DEVELOPING STEM LCK IN PRACTICE

In the remaining sections, we illustrate the process of building LCK to support leaders in providing rich, actionable feedback to teachers in STEM. First, we highlight examples of concepts or practices central to mathematics and science instruction. Second, we share two LCK Challenge iterations, one in mathematics and one in science. Finally, we model how an existing structure can be used to build STEM LCK and enhance the supervisory experience.

Core Concepts/Instructional Practices for Postholing in Mathematics

In mathematics, the National Council of Teachers of Mathematics (NCTM, 2014) outlines eight effective teaching practices. These eight practices come together to form a "non-negotiable core" of "research-informed actions for all teachers, coaches, and specialists in mathematics; all school and district administrators; and all educational leaders and policymakers" (NCTM, 2014, p. 4). Figure 8.2 introduces the eight effective teaching practices, demonstrating how they are related to each other. NCTM (2014) elaborates on all eight practices, providing research base for, illustration of, and student and teacher actions that align with each.

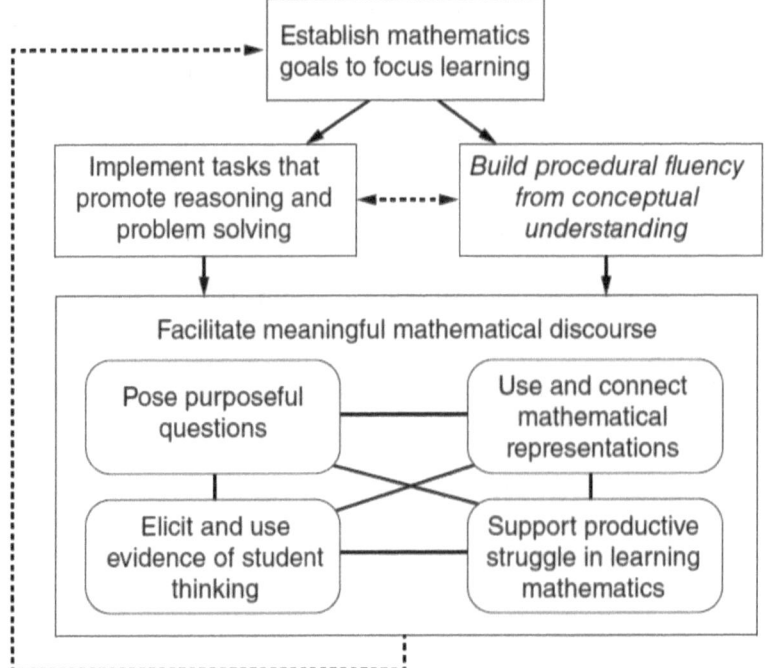

Figure 8.2. The relationships between the eight effective teaching practices

Source: Reprinted with permission from *Taking Action: Implementing Effective Mathematics Teaching Practices in Grades 6–8,* ©2017, by the National Council of Teachers of Mathematics. All rights reserved.

Three of these practices provide an initial foray into understanding and visualizing ambitious mathematics instruction.

- Implement tasks that promote reasoning and problem solving. Effective teaching of mathematics engages students in solving and discussing tasks that promote mathematics reasoning and problem solving and allow multiple entry points and varied solution strategies.
- Build procedural fluency from conceptual understanding. Effective teaching of mathematics builds fluency with procedures in a foundation of conceptual understanding so that students, over time, become skillful in using procedures flexibly as they solve contextual and mathematical problems.
- Facilitate meaningful mathematical discourse. Effective teaching of mathematics facilitates discourse among students to build shared understanding of mathematical ideas by analyzing and comparing student approaches and arguments. (NCTM, 2014, p. 10)

In conjunction, these three practices paint a picture of the activity in a mathematics classroom. Students are productively struggling with high-level tasks providing students the opportunity to reason conceptually about the mathematics, share their reasoning with others, listen to the thinking of their peers, evaluate such thinking, and contrast an array of approaches.

Instead of using a *funneling* questioning pattern that directs students to follow a certain procedure or arrive at a particular answer, teachers should use a *focusing* questioning pattern that centers on student thinking, supports students in communicating their ideas, and orients students to the evaluation of each other's mathematical reasoning (Herbel-Eisenmann & Breyfogle, 2005). Therefore, when observing mathematics teachers, school leaders need to move beyond identifying the presence of questions to attending to the intention and outcomes of the discourse patterns in a classroom.

Preparing for and engaging in pre- and postobservation dialogues centered on these effective practices builds LCK and opens the opportunity for discipline-specific feedback. Table 8.1 illustrates how coaching stems can be adjusted for mathematics instruction.

Table 8.1. Example coaching stems/prompts: Mathematics

Core/Focal Practice	Phase	Potential Coaching Questions
Implement tasks that promote reasoning and problem solving	Preobservation	In what task(s) will students engage? How do you anticipate students will solve the task (correct conceptions and misconceptions)?
	Postobservation	What kinds of approaches did you observe students taking regarding the tasks? Were there approaches you anticipated?
Build procedural fluency from conceptual understanding	Preobservation	What have you set up in the lesson/unit to enable students to develop and demonstrate procedural fluency from conceptual knowledge?
	Postobservation	How are students demonstrating their conceptual understanding and procedural fluency? What are your next steps to support the diversity of student thinking?
Facilitate meaningful mathematical discourse	Preobservation	What structures or approaches will you use to facilitate meaningful mathematical discourse during the lesson?
	Postobservation	What prompts, questions, or actions did you use to encourage students to talk and listen to one another? How did you encourage reluctant learners to participate in the class discussion?

Core Concepts/Instructional Practices for Postholing in Science

In *A Framework for K–12 Science Education: Practices, Crosscutting Concepts, and Core Ideas*, the National Research Council (NRC, 2012) outlines three key dimensions that are critical to developing scientific literacy: scientific practices, crosscutting concepts, and disciplinary core ideas.

An initial examination of three (of the eight) scientific practices helps leaders understand what they should see and hear with regularity in a science classroom:

- *Planning and carrying out investigations.* Scientists design and implement experiments, attending to controlling variables and what constitutes scientific data.
- *Developing and using models.* Scientists create models to communicate understandings of processes and structures in nature. Models can be simple representations of observable phenomena or more complex representations of abstract or theoretical explanations.
- *Engaging in argument from evidence.* Scientists engage in arguments based on empirical evidence and test adequacy of competing explanations of natural phenomena.

One way to incorporate science practices into instruction is the 5E Model (Bybee et al., 2006).

With the 5E model, teachers (E)ngage students by posing problems to expose students to novel phenomena, setting the stage for the (E)xplore phase for which students investigate objects, design experiments, and create models. Students then (E)xplain what they have discovered about the phenomena in their own words and share evidence to justify explanations. During the (E)laborate phase, students connect their newfound knowledge to prior concepts and apply new academic language and skills to different but similar situations. Finally, teachers (E)valuate the effectiveness of the cycle by assessing student learning in a variety of ways.

The second dimension emphasized by the framework is the seven crosscutting concepts: patterns; cause and effect; scale, proportion, and quantity; systems and system models; energy and matter; structure and function; and stability and change (NRC, 2012). These concepts "bridge disciplinary boundaries" in science, serve as an "organizational framework for connecting knowledge from various disciplines," and help students develop a "coherent and scientifically based view of the world" (NRC, 2012, p. 83).

Finally, core scientific ideas, like the nature of science (NOS), should be cornerstones of quality science instruction. NOS aspects include the following (Binns & Bloom, 2017; Lederman, 2007):

- *Evidence.* Scientific claims must be based upon empirical evidence.
- *Observations and inferences.* Scientific knowledge is derived from observations of evidence (empirical) as well as inferential explanations of the evidence (theoretical).
- *Tentativeness.* Scientific claims are subject to change with new evidence or technology.
- *Social and cultural influences.* Societal and cultural values guide or restrict the types of questions asked and investigations conducted.
- *Natural causes.* Science is limited to *natural* causes to explain phenomena in nature.

By emphasizing these aspects of NOS, teachers help students develop a more sophisticated understanding of science, increase their confidence in science, and guide the distinction between scientific and unscientific claims (Bloom, 2021; Binns & Bloom, 2017; Lederman, 2007).

Preparing for and engaging in pre- and postobservation dialogues centered on these practices and concepts provides a constructive anchor for supervising science teachers while building LCK. Table 8.2 illustrates how coaching stems can be adjusted for science instruction.

Example of the LCK Challenge in Mathematics

A school leader who takes on the LCK Challenge to build knowledge in the area of learning and teaching mathematics could first join the organization National Council of Teachers of Mathematics (NCTM). With the NCTM membership, the school leader will receive the journal, *Mathematics Teacher: Learning and Teaching PK–12*. Additionally, the school leader plans to attend one of NCTM's regional conferences with several teachers.

The school leader also seeks recommendations for two books to read from the campus mathematics specialist. The school leader decides to read *Principles to Actions: Ensuring Mathematical Success for All* (NCTM, 2014) for an introduction to effective teaching practices for the mathematics classroom. For the second book, the school leader chooses *5 Practices for Orchestrating Productive Mathematics Discussions* (Smith & Stein, 2018). This book provides a framework to structure a lesson integrating the effective teaching practices (figure 8.2).

Example of the LCK Challenge in Science

Similarly, a school leader could take on the LCK Challenge to deepen their knowledge about the learning and teaching of science. After becoming a member of the National Science Teaching Association (NSTA), a school

Table 8.2. Example coaching stems/prompts: Science

Core/Focal Practice	Phase	Potential Coaching Questions
Planning and carrying out investigations	Preobservation	In what experiments or activities will students engage? How much will students be involved in the design of experiments?
	Postobservation	What procedural or conceptual errors did students encounter and/or overcome as they worked through the activity/experiment? How might you address those?
Developing and using models	Preobservation	How will models be utilized in the lesson to explain natural phenomena?
	Postobservation	How did you ensure that students understood the concepts depicted by the model? How might you involve students in developing similar models?
Engaging in argument from evidence	Preobservation	What conflicts or tensions could arise between the content in this lesson and the personal beliefs of students? How do you plan to navigate those?
	Postobservation	What examples of weak or inappropriate connections between arguments/responses and empirical evidence did students make? What are your next steps with these students?

leader has access to *Interactive eBooks for Professional Learning*, which will help deepen content knowledge across myriad science topics; monthly professional learning web seminars hosted by science education specialists as well as practicing scientists; discounted registration to the NSTA national conference; and five journals focusing on science teaching (e.g., *Science and Children, Science Scope, The Science Teacher*).

Membership also provides a discount for NSTA Press publications, including books a school leader can reads as part of the LCK Challenge. *The NSTA Reader's Guide to a Framework for K–12 Science Education* (Pratt, 2016) identifies core ideas of each science discipline, reveals crosscutting concepts, and unpacks science and engineering practices (NRC, 2012). A complementary book is *Helping Students Make Sense of the World Using Next Generation Science and Engineering Practices* (Schwarz et al., 2017), which communicates how to effectively incorporate the eight science and engineering practices into practice.

Reframing Existing Structures

One way to reframe existing district structures is to *use artifacts* (e.g., observation and evaluation rubrics) *as springboards for discussion* around high-quality, discipline-focused teaching practices. School leaders often use evaluation rubrics to assess teachers' instruction. So that the rubric can be used across disciplines, the descriptors and indicators of the various domains of evaluation are often presented in content-neutral language.

To build STEM LCK, school leaders can adapt a school's tools of supervision based on knowledge gained from the LCK Challenge or in collaboration with colleagues or content-area experts. Leaders select a portion of a supervision instrument and revise content-neutral items to reflect STEM discipline-based standards and pedagogy. Leaders can then apply the refined tool to observe and provide actionable feedback to a teacher in a STEM field. Table 8.3 shows the adaptation of Dimension 2.3—Communication of the Texas Teacher Evaluation & Support System (T-TESS) to reflect research-based practices in mathematics and science (TEA, 2022).

CONCLUSION

Instructional leadership is not an easy task, but the pathway to becoming a stronger instructional leader begins with intentional, consistent practices to learn about STEM content and pedagogies. The present chapter shares and models approaches to developing STEM LCK. By self-assessing areas in which leaders need to build their STEM LCK, they can purposefully design their own LCK Challenge and leverage existing district structures. In time, they position themselves to support teachers in STEM disciplines through providing credible and actionable feedback grounded in research-based practices.

POSTREADING REFLECTIONS/ACTIVITIES

- Plan your own LCK Challenge.
  - Choose a focal area in the STEM disciplines (e.g., science, technology, engineering, or mathematics) and dig into the standards and evidence-based practices associated with that focal area. Use figure 8.1 to help plan out your action steps.
  - Engage a collaborator or mentor with whom you can debrief.
  - Report out to faculty at regular intervals. This helps you process information, demonstrates your commitment to deepening your understanding related to STEM instruction and can build credibility with STEM teachers.

Table 8.3. Indicators of Dimension 2.3–Communication from the T-TESS Revised to Reflect Mathematics and Science Practices (TEA, 2022)

Distinguished Indicators	Mathematics Practices	Science Practices

Establishes classroom practices that encourage all students to communicate safely and effectively using a variety of tools and methods with the teacher and their peers.	Fosters "an academically safe classroom [that] honors the individual as a mathematician and welcomes him or her into the social ecosystem of math" (Krall, 2018, p. 20) by
	1. positioning *all* students as capable of doing mathematics through challenging status (e.g., perceived smartness) and marginalization of students (NCTM, 2018, p. 33), and
	2. building norms around discourse that situate students as "authors of ideas," who (NCTM, 2014, p. 35):
	  • explain and justify their thinking;
	  • critically listen to, ask follow-up questions, evaluate, and describe the thinking of others; and
	  • attempt, compare, and contrast various strategies.
		Makes student engagement in guided inquiry projects (including scientific investigations) a regular and central classroom practice. Students are:
		1. collaborating with peers to develop and enact experiments to seek understanding of natural phenomena,
		2. revising their experiments when necessary, and
		3. communicating their findings (explain) to others in order to demonstrate their developing understanding based upon their findings (Bybee et al., 2006).

Uses possible student misunderstandings as strategic points in lessons to highlight misconceptions and inspire exploration and discovery.	Establishes an environment in which students understand that confusion and mistakes are integral to learning by 1. providing students with opportunities to productively struggle with the mathematics and persevere in solving problems; 2. anticipating potential misconceptions and challenges; and 3. preparing questions and counterexamples to make errors and misunderstandings visible and facilitate conversations to examine them (NCTM, 2014, pp. 48, 52, 54).	Guides students in enacting the practices of science so they can "build, test, evaluate, and refine knowledge" (*Reiser et al., 2013, p. 73): 1. explore, rephrase, and test correct and incorrect conceptions (NSTA, 2017), and 2. use data to explain how the competing explanations were generated and why, ultimately, one persisted over the other(s).
Provides explanations that are clear and coherent and uses verbal and written communication that is clear and correct.	Avoids imprecise language and overgeneralized tips or tricks (e.g., carry, borrow, FOIL) and instead use precise mathematical language grounded in conceptual mathematical understanding (e.g., trade, regroup, distributive property) (Karp et al., 2014, 2015).	1. Uses models to communicate complex scientific concepts, emphasizing that models are only approximations of the actual phenomena and are limited simplifications used to explain them (*Krajcik & Merritt, 2013). 2. Aids students in acquiring academic language, replacing everyday vocabulary with correct scientific terms. 3. Distinguishes meaning behind informal and scientific use of words such as hypothesis, theory, and law (NRC, 2012).

Asks questions at the creative, evaluative and/or analysis levels that require a deeper understanding of the objective of the lesson.	Includes all four types of questions used in mathematics instruction: 1. Gathering information 2. Probing thinking 3. Making the mathematics visible 4. Encouraging reflection and justification (NCTM, 2014, pp. 36–37)	Guides student-led inquiry activities (*Bybee, 2013) Asks questions such as: 1. What is your evidence? 2. How can we test that claim? 3. Why did you get that result? 4. What does your data tell you? 5. How would you redesign your experiment? (NRC, 2012)
Skillfully balances wait time, questioning techniques and integration of student responses to support student-directed learning.	Uses a *focusing* discourse pattern that incorporates wait time, centers on student thinking, encourages students to clearly articulate their reasoning, directs students to the ideas of their peers, and fosters student-to-student talk (NCTM, 2014, pp. 37, 41).	Gives students the opportunity to share understanding gained from their guided inquiry experience, based upon the data they collected. If necessary, clarifies student explanations with direct instruction and addresses any misconceptions (Bybee et al., 2006).
Skillfully provokes and guides discussion to pique curiosity and inspire student-led learning of meaningful and challenging content.	Employs the 5 Practices for Orchestrating Productive Mathematics Discussions (Smith & Stein, 2018) to prepare for and implement a lesson centered on student thinking: 0. Set goals and select high-level tasks 1. Anticipate student strategies for solving the task 2. Monitor students working on the task 3. Select student strategies to be shared 4. Sequence the selected strategies for student presentations and discussion 5. Connect student strategies to each other and the mathematical goals of the lesson (NCTM, 2014, p. 30)	1. Invites students to generate questions that are relevant to their lives. 2. Poses scenarios or identifies a problem that students can investigate (Bybee, et al., 2006). 3. Stimulates curiosity by demonstrating a discrepant event that surprises or confuses students (Lederman & Abd-el-Khalick, 1998). 4. Guides students to apply their newfound understanding to broader and unrelated contexts (Bybee et al., 2006).

Note: * indicates that the reference is from Pratt (2016).

- Examine whatever evaluation or supervision tools are used in your district.
  - Select a portion of the instrument and, given what you learn in the LCK Challenge, add discipline-specific indicators to guide what you notice/look for in a STEM classroom. Collaborate with an expert teacher or instructional specialist in this effort.
  - After revising a portion of the instrument, use it in some observations or walkthroughs as well as the follow-up debriefs with teachers. Reflect on how your noticings and dialogues with teachers changed when supported by your growing knowledge of the discipline and discipline-specific instructional strategies.

REFERENCES

Binns, I. C., & Bloom, M. A. (2017). Using nature of science to mitigate tension in teaching evolution. In Lynn, C. D., Glaze, A. L., Evans, W. A., & Reed, L. K. (Eds.), *Evolution education in the American South: Culture, politics, and resources in and around Alabama* (pp. 135–46). Palgrave Macmillan.

Bloom, M. A. (2021). The links between the virtues, science and science education. In Melville, W. & Kerr, D. (Eds.), *Virtues as integral to science education: Understanding the intellectual, moral, and civic value of science and scientific inquiry.* Routledge.

Bybee, R. W. (2013). Scientific and engineering practices in K–12 classrooms. In Pratt, H. (Ed.), *The NSTA reader's guide to A Framework for K–12 Science Education.* NSTA Press.

Bybee, R. W., Taylor, J. A., Cardner, A., Van Scotter, P., Powell, J. C., Westbrook, A., & Landes, N. (2006). The BSCS 5E instructional model: Origins and effectiveness. BSCS. https://bscs.org/wp-content/uploads/2022/01/bscs_5e_full_report-1.pdf

Cunningham, K. M. W., & Lochmiller, C. R. (2020). Content-specific leadership: Identifying literature-based implications for principal preparation. *Journal of Research on Leadership Education 15*(4), 261–82. https://doi.org/10.1177/2F1942775119845004

Ford, T. G., Lavigne, A. L., Fiegener, A. M., & Si, S. (2020). Understanding district support for leader development and success in the accountability era: A review of the literature using social-cognitive theories of motivation. *Review of Educational Research 90*(2), 264–307. https://doi.org/10.3102%2F0034654319899723

Fullan, M. (2016). *The new meaning of educational change* (5th ed.). Teachers College Press.

Glickman, C. D., Gordon, S. P., & Ross-Gordon, J. M. (2017). *SuperVision and instructional leadership: A developmental approach.* Pearson.

Herbel-Eisenmann, B. A., & Breyfogle, M. L. (2005). Questioning our patterns of questioning. *Mathematics Teaching in the Middle School, 10*(9), 484–89.

Hitt, D. H., & Tucker, P. D. (2016). Systematic review of key leader practices found to influence student achievement: A unified framework. *Review of Educational Research, 86*(2), 531–69. https://doi.org/10.3102%2F0034654315614911

Jimerson, J. B., & Quebec Fuentes, S. (2021a). Approaches to instructional leadership: Organizational influences in contexts of (mis)match. *Journal of School Leadership 31*(4), 343–67. https://doi.org/10.1177%2F1052684620980359

Jimerson, J. B., & Quebec Fuentes, S. (2021b, October). Empowering principals with LCK: Reframing district structures can bolster instructional leadership. *The Learning Principal.* https://learningforward.org/journal/leadership-under-pressure/online-exclusive-how-principals-lead-across-content-areas/

Karp, K. S., Bush, S. B., & Dougherty, B. J. (2014). 13 rules that expire. *Teaching Children Mathematics, 21*(1), 18–25.

Karp, K. S., Bush, S. B., & Dougherty, B. J. (2015). 12 math rules that expire in the middle grades. *Mathematics Teaching in the Middle School, 21*(4), 208–15.

Krall, G. (2018). *Necessary conditions: Teaching secondary math with academic safety, quality tasks, and effective facilitation.* Stenhouse Publishers.

Lederman, N. G. (2007). Nature of science: Past, present, and future. In Abell, S. K., & Lederman, N. G. (Eds.), *Handbook of research on science education.* Lawrence Erlbaum Associates Inc.

Lederman, N. G., & Abd-el-Khalick, F. (1998). Avoiding de-natured science: Activities that promote understandings of the nature of science. In McComas, W. F. (Ed.), *The nature of science in science education.* Kluwer Academic Publishers.

Lochmiller, C. R. (2016). Examining administrators' instructional feedback to high school math and science teachers. *Educational Administration Quarterly, 52*(1), 75–109. https://doi.org/10.1177%2F0013161X15616660

Lochmiller, C. R., & Acker-Hocevar, M. (2016). Making sense of principal leadership in content areas: The case of secondary math and science instruction. *Leadership and Policy in Schools, 15*(3), 273–96. https://doi.org/10.1080/15700763.2015.1073329

National Council of Teachers of Mathematics (NCTM). (2014). *Principals to actions: Ensuring mathematical success for all.* Author.

National Council of Teachers of Mathematics (NCTM). (2018). *Catalyzing change in high school mathematics: Initiating critical conversations.* Author.

National Research Council (NRC). (2012). *A framework for K–12 science education: Practices, crosscutting concepts, and core ideas.* National Academies Press.

National Science Teacher Association (NSTA). (2017). *Helping students make sense of the world using Next Generation Science and Engineering Practices.* NSTA Press.

Pratt, H. (2016). *The NSTA reader's guide to a framework for K–12 science education: Practices, crosscutting concepts, and core ideas.* NSTA Press.

Quebec Fuentes, S., & Jimerson, J. B. (2020). Role enactment and types of feedback: The influence of leadership content knowledge on instructional leadership efforts. *Journal of Educational Supervision 3*(2), 6–31. https://doi.org/10.31045/jes.3.2.2

Quebec Fuentes, S., & Jimerson, J. B. (2019). Tackling instructional mismatch: Targeted, intentional learning can build leaders' content knowledge. *The Learning Professional 40*(5), 32–35.

Schwarz, C. V., Passmore, C., & Reiser, B. J. (2017). *Helping students make sense of the world using next generation science and engineering practices.* NSTA Press.

Smith, M. S., Steele, M. D., & Raithe, M. L. (2017). *Taking action: Implementing effective mathematics teaching practices in grades 6-8.* NCTM.

Smith, M. S., & Stein, M. K. (2018). *5 practices for orchestrating productive mathematics discussions.* NCTM.

Stein, M. K., & Nelson, B. S. (2003). Leadership content knowledge. *Educational Evaluation and Policy Analysis, 25*(4), 423–48. https://doi.org/10.3102%2F01623737025004423

Texas Education Association (TEA). (2022). *T-TESS rubric.* https://teachfortexas.org/Resource_Files/Guides/T-TESS_Rubric.pdf

CHAPTER 9

Research-based Supervision and Feedback Practices in Literacy Instruction

Janice A. Dole, Parker C. Fawson, and D. Ray Reutzel

PREFOCUS GUIDING QUESTIONS

- What are the foundations for effective literacy instruction?
- How can clinical supervision and feedback be used to improve and evaluate literacy instruction?
- How can literacy coaches, professional learning communities, and technology be used to improve the supervision and feedback of literacy instruction?

INTRODUCTION

Developing proficiency in literacy forms the foundation upon which a child can build a flourishing life. It establishes the footing for knowledge growth, which then can activate a life filled with opportunity that can be animated by the successful reader. Castles et al. (2018) argued, "Learning to read transforms lives. Reading is the basis for the acquisition of knowledge, for cultural engagement, for democracy, and for success in the workplace" (p. 5).

For much of the past century, educators, parents, and policy makers have argued over how to best teach children to read. Sadly, these often-heated disagreements, which morphed into the "reading wars" in the later decades of the 1900s, produced confusion among the educational community in the United States.

The "reading wars" has led to the continued distraction away from the research that clearly delineates what students need to learn to be successful readers. This knowledge base is called the "Science of Reading"—"the accumulated knowledge about reading, reading development, and best practices for reading instruction obtained through the use of the scientific method" (Petscher et al., 2020, p. S268).

Research that undergirds the science of reading is grounded in the fields of developmental psychology, educational psychology, cognitive science, and cognitive neurosciences (Reutzel & Fawson, 2021). Data supporting what we know about proficient reading and how to teach it well have been emerging for over a century. The knowledge base is also informing effective instructional practices that hold great promise in supporting young children as they develop into proficient readers.

Castles et al. (2018) suggest that to achieve the core goal of reading as being able to understand text, three core considerations emerge out of the science of reading that must be present in our reading instruction. These three broad instructional categories include

- cracking the alphabetic code
- acquiring fluent word-recognition capacity
- comprehending text

Additionally, literacy teachers have refined their instruction to better align with the learning expectations identified in the Common Core State Standards (CCSS; Common Core State Standards Initiative, 2010). These standards identify grade-level expectations for student learning in reading, writing, and language. Since literacy is a central attribute for animating a life of opportunity and flourishing, the CCSS provides specific guidance for students' English language arts (ELA) learning trajectories.

Effective literacy instruction will help students develop competency in the three areas mentioned by Castles et al. (2018) while also targeting CCSS (2010) grade-level expectations. Instructional strategies that achieve these outcomes should be embedded in a coherent, knowledge-based curriculum that introduces students to challenging and knowledge-rich narrative and informational texts to increase the likelihood that students have the prerequisite knowledge to ensure learning advantages persist into later learning opportunities and throughout their lives (Wexler, 2020; Willingham, 2017).

All students benefit from learning that introduces them to the weighty content and rich knowledge that describes the world in which they live. Proficient reading ability allows each student to take full advantage of knowledge that can be acquired through accessing complex and challenging text that opens their thinking up to disciplines like world and US history, Greek mythology, and science.

School leaders must understand that literacy proficiency is not acquired for its own sake but for expanding students' knowledge of their world (Reutzel & Fawson, 2021; Reutzel et al., 2005). Good examples of knowledge-based curricula include Amplify's *Core Knowledge* and Great Mind's *Wit and Wisdom*.

SUPERVISION AND FEEDBACK TO IMPROVE LITERACY

How do school leaders know good literacy instruction when they see it in classrooms? What does it look or sound like? School leaders knowledgeable in the science of reading (SOR) understand the components of a strong reading program and use frequent clinical supervision and feedback visits to classrooms to assist teachers in implementing high-quality literacy instruction.

Clinical Supervision

Focused attention and feedback related to teaching literacy comes from an understanding of SOR and the instruction that occurs in support of SOR. "Clinical supervision," refers to a process whereby supervisory observations with feedback lead to improved teaching expertise (Marzano et al., 2011).

The process of clinical supervision begins with a planning conference in which school leaders—principals, coaches, peers—and teachers discuss an upcoming lesson. For example, suppose a school leader plans to observe a first-grade phonics lesson. The leader would preview the lesson to see if the teacher's knowledge of phonics is consistent with SOR. The teacher may ask the school leader to look for teacher clarity in how she communicates her lesson to students and whether students understand what they are learning and why they are learning it.

As the school leader observes the lesson, she takes notes focusing particular attention on teacher clarity—whether the teacher clearly explains how the sounds connect to the letters. The school leader may talk to individual students to see if they understand what they are learning and why. After the lesson, the teacher and school leader debrief about the lesson, paying particular attention to whether students understood the lesson and which students will require further instruction.

Classroom Observation Tools

Clinical supervision of literacy instruction is aided by classroom observation tools that provide school leaders and teachers with the critical attributes of the effective teaching of literacy. Marzano et al. (2011) and Sullivan and Glanz (2013) have accumulated a host of observation tools for classroom observations. Many of these tools can easily be adapted to relate specifically to SOR.

One type of observation tool used extensively by school leaders is checklists. Checklists provide school leaders with helpful guides to effective literacy instruction.

To help school leaders know what to look for, we highly recommend that school leaders use one of the following observation guide/checklists: the Institute of Education Sciences' K–3 Schools Leaders Literacy Walkthrough and/or the Guide and Checklists for a School Leader's Walkthrough During Literacy Instruction in Grades 4–12 (https://ies.ed.gov/ncee/edLabs/regions/southeast/inc/docs/School_Leaders_Literacy_Walkthrough_Kindergarten_First_Second_and_Third_Grades.pdf; https://ies.ed.gov/ncee/edlabs/regions/southeast/pdf/REL_2020018.pdf).

Another type of observation tool comes in the form of rubrics. Rubrics can provide a more complex analysis of a school and classroom literacy program. We recommend the Consortium on Reading Excellence in Education (CORE; http://www.corelearn.com/wp-content/uploads/2016/10/ela-implementation-rubric-core.pdf) for a thorough guide for school leaders to evaluate the overall quality of literacy instruction at the school and classroom level.

Formal Observation Tools

While informal checklists and rubrics can help develop teacher expertise in reading and literacy, it cannot be assumed that these checklists and rubrics include all those critical attributes that lead to improved literacy achievement. It is worthwhile to examine observation tools that have been empirically demonstrated to impact not only teacher expertise, but student achievement as well. Three popular observation tool systems with a solid research base are,

- The *Classroom Assessment Scoring System* (CLASS; Pianta et al., 2003)
- *Framework for Teaching* (Danielson, 2006)
- *Protocol for Language Arts Teaching Observations* (PLATO; Grossman et al., 2013)

The first two systems are generic tools that address what Shulman (1987) calls "pedagogical knowledge"; that knowledge about instructional practices that leads to teacher expertise in any subject area. For example, teacher expertise improves when teachers provide clear expectations and effective engagement (Pianta et al., 2003).

PLATO (Grossman et al., 2013) addresses this pedagogical knowledge, but it also addresses Shulman's (1987) "pedagogical content knowledge," which is the knowledge about *how to teach literacy*. For example, PLATO includes teaching for "depth of understanding," which is pedagogical knowledge, but it also includes "modeling how to write a summary," which is specific pedagogical content knowledge about literacy.

Thus, PLATO (Grossman et al., 2013) is a research-based observation tool that addresses the pedagogical and pedagogical content knowledge necessary to improve literacy instruction and achievement. While checklists, rubrics, and other observation tools can be useful in supervision and feedback, formal systems like PLATO have been demonstrated to *improve student achievement*—the holy grail of clinical supervision.

Feedback to Support Teacher Growth

In clinical supervision, effective feedback is critical to teacher growth and development. The goal of feedback is to promote self-reflective teachers who can assess their own teaching. However, new teachers may need specific guidance to develop into self-reflective learners. For example, when asked, "Were all your students able to summarize a paragraph based on your lesson?" new teachers may not know, or they may be incorrect in their assessment. They may need specific guidance in strategies for assessing student understanding at the completion of a lesson.

Feedback that is reflective is often most helpful for teachers with teaching experience. Many of these teachers can pinpoint problems in their literacy lessons without help from a school leader. School leaders can ask these questions:

- How well did students work together collaboratively on your summarization lesson? Were they able to help one another in their task?
- What happened when you asked students to summarize a paragraph on their own?
- Were students ready to do this task on their own? How do you know?
- "What do you need to do next?

Expert teachers can generally pinpoint strengths of their lessons, identify which parts were not understood well by students, and what teachers can do in the next lesson to improve student understanding.

LITERACY LEADERSHIP TO IMPROVE LITERACY INSTRUCTION

Traditionally, school leaders and administrators—most often the principal—served as primary supervisors and evaluators of teachers. However, in recent years supervision and feedback has been decoupled from evaluation, and new methods of supporting literacy instruction have taken the place of the school principal as supervisor. In fact, research has demonstrated that effective schools distribute power among a team of school-based leaders to develop teacher expertise in an ongoing effort to improve student literacy outcomes (Wohlstetter & Malloy, 2001).

Team-Based Learning to Extend Literacy Supervision and Feedback: Professional Development Communities

Rentfro (2007) asserts that a professional learning community (PLC) model gives schools a framework to build teacher expertise and leadership capacity to work as members of high-performing, collaborative teams that focus on improving student learning, including literacy. Wise school leaders support team-based learning and leadership development because it is often the teachers who remain in their positions at a school and can sustain or undermine long-term and real instructional change.

Professional learning communities are defined as educators committed to working collaboratively in ongoing processes of collective inquiry and action research to achieve better results for the students they serve. PLCs operate under the assumption that the key to improved learning for students is continuous, job-embedded learning (DuFour & DuFour, 2006). Successful literacy-focused PLCs include the following:

- Establishing a shared literacy mission (purpose), vision (clear direction), values (collective commitments), and goals (indicators, timelines, and targets)
- Working to create a shared commitment to guiding principles that articulate what the staff in the school believe and what they seek to accomplish in literacy instruction
- Focusing on student literacy learning as the most valued outcome
- Creating collective commitments to clarify what each member of the staff will do to contribute to accomplishing results-oriented literacy goals
- Promoting organizational renewal and a willingness of staff to work together in a continuous literacy instruction improvement process
- Collaborating as a *systemic* process where staff work together interdependently to analyze and impact literacy instructional and assessment practices in order to improve results for students, the team, and the school's literacy culture
- Engaging in regular collective inquiry into best, evidence-based literacy practices and current reality
- Supporting and sustaining an action orientation
- Expecting high-literacy-learning results—no excuses.

School leaders can effectively extend their capacity as supervisors through establishing and participating in productive literacy focused PLCs that frequently and thoughtfully examine literacy instruction practices, programs, and assessment as these impact student progress toward literacy proficiency targets.

Literacy Coaches: Extending Supervision and Feedback

Over the last 20 years, some of the leadership of literacy programs has come from literacy coaches. A meta-analysis on coaching research found that "teacher coaching has large positive effects on both instructional practice and student achievement" (Kraft et al., 2018, p. 71). Literacy coaches can mentor, supervise, and support literacy teachers to improve their literacy knowledge and skill in assessment planning, instructional delivery, and use of student literacy data. They can collect and communicate information efficiently and effectively.

Effective literacy coaches and school leaders provide affirmative, corrective, and evaluative feedback to teachers on the effectiveness of their literacy instruction. Literacy coaches must have specialized knowledge, expertise, and demonstrated accomplishment in literacy instruction to do this (L'Allier et al., 2010).

Literacy coaches and school leaders should familiarize themselves with the *International Literacy Association's 2017 Standards for the Preparation of Specialized Literacy Professionals*—for classroom teachers at the following website: https://www.literacyworldwide.org/docs/default-source/resource-documents/standards-appendix-C.pdf. For example, ILA Standard 2.2: Curriculum and Instruction, which states,

> teachers plan, modify, and implement evidence-based and integrated instructional approaches that develop reading processes as related to foundational skills (concepts of print, phonological awareness, phonics, word recognition, and fluency), vocabulary, and comprehension for elementary/early primary grade learners.

If we were observing in a first-grade classroom using *The School Leaders' Literacy Walkthrough Guide for 1st grade*, we would find the Foundational Reading Skills, Grade 1 checklist. If the teacher to be observed was scheduled to teach a phonological awareness lesson, the look-fors found in this checklist might be:

- Distinguish long from short vowels sounds in spoken single-syllable words
- Orally produce single-syllable words by blending individual speech sounds (e.g., /s/ /i/ /t/–sit)

- Segment spoken single-syllable words into their sequence of individual sounds (e.g., mat–/m/ /a/ /t/)

Another example might involve ILA Standard 5.4: Learners and the Literacy Environment, which states, "Candidates create physical and social literacy-rich environments that use routines and a variety of grouping configurations for independent and collaborative learning."

If we were observing in a fifth-grade classroom using the *IES Guide and Checklists for a School Leaders' Walkthrough During Literacy Instruction in Grades 4–12*, we would find the Grades 4 and 5 Whole Class Literacy Checklist. If the teacher to be observed was scheduled to teach a comprehension lesson, the look-fors found in this checklist might be:

- Small-group instructional interventions are provided to English learner students and others who are struggling with literacy skills and English language development
- Small-group (3–5 students) instruction is differentiated, focusing on areas of need
- Instruction includes extensive opportunities for students to encounter and comprehend grade-level text
- Opportunities are provided for students to discuss texts in whole and small groups
- A discussion protocol has been developed and is being implemented
- A print-rich literacy classroom learning environment
- Conditions in the classroom promote higher reading engagement and conceptual learning through strategies such as goal setting, self-directed learning, and collaborative learning

School leaders need to focus the work of the literacy coach and classroom teachers squarely on improved instructional quality that leads to student literacy proficiency. Finally, school leaders also make sure they are generous in their support of professional learning opportunities to help literacy coaches continue their own professional learning and development.

Using Technology to Extend Supervision and Feedback

During and after the COVID-19 pandemic, school leaders, PLCs, and literacy coaches found a variety of ways to support literacy teachers to leverage the power of technology in their literacy instruction. For example, some teachers adapted technology to provide students with effective online student read-aloud experiences (Stoetzel & Shedrow, 2021). They provided multimedia displays of literacy skills and lesson content using digital white boards to display text, videos, graphic arts, and websites, as well as to access audio (voice and music) to support in-class and online reading lessons.

Technology is increasingly used to support the professional growth of literacy teachers. During and after the pandemic, many elementary teachers have joined virtual professional communities of practice (VPLCs) online to receive professional development. For example, Baxa and Christ (2017) developed the *DigiLit Framework* to help teachers make thoughtful choices about the effective selection and integration of digital texts/tools into literacy lessons.

Literacy coaches can meet with their teachers online to receive continued professional development, e-supervision, and e-feedback on submitted examples of online instruction and lessons (Fisher & Frey, 2020; Ippolito & Bean, 2021). Teachers can also stay in touch with one another professionally through e-book clubs, social media, and discussions of e-case studies.

Finally, professional organizations such as the International Literacy Association have made a host of digital literacy resources available to support teachers and coaches. These organizations continue to innovate ways for leaders, teachers, and coaches to learn together, even when they are separated by unusual circumstances or great distances.

CONCLUSION

Research into effective literacy instruction has provided a rich source of information about high-quality literacy learning and its instruction. Research on supervision and instruction has added new models of supervision— observation tools, rubrics, and systems to support effective literacy instruction and provide effective feedback to teachers.

New models of literacy leadership have also emerged in the form of PLCs, coaching, and technology. It seems clear that these new models are an improvement over the traditional evaluation models of the past. How these new models impact literacy achievement in the future remains a question for the next several decades.

POSTREADING REFLECTIONS/ACTIVITIES

- Observe a phonics lesson of a first-year teacher and an expert teacher using *The School Leaders' Literacy Walkthrough Guide for 1st grade*. Draft two outlines of potential feedback you would give to each teacher based on what you have learned in this chapter.
- How can school leaders use professional learning communities to promote teachers' learning about the science of reading?

REFERENCES

Baxa, J., & Christ, T. (2017). The DigiLit framework. *The Reading Teacher, 71*(6), 703-14. https://doi:10.1002/trtr.1660

Castles, A., Rastle, K., & Nation, K. (2018). Ending the reading wars: Reading acquisition from novice to expert. *Psychological Science in the Public Interest, 19*(1), 5-51. https://doi: 10.1177/1529100618772271

Common Core State Standards Initiative. (2010). *Common Core State Standards for English language arts and literacy in history, social studies, science, and technical subjects.* Council of Chief State School Officers & National Governors Association. http://www.corestandards.org/ELA-Literacy

Danielson, C. (2006). *Teacher leadership that strengthens professional practice.* Association for Supervision and Curriculum Development.

DuFour, R., & DuFour, R. (2006). The power of professional learning communities. *National Forum of Educational Administration and Supervision Journal, 24*(1), 2-5.

Fisher, D., & Frey, N. (2020). Lessons from pandemic teaching for content area literacy. *The Reading Teacher, 74*(3), 341-345. https://doi.org/10.1002/trtr.1947

Grossman, P., Loeb, S., Cohen, J., & Wyckoff, J. (2013). Measure for measure: The relationship between measures of instructional practice in middle school English language arts and teachers' value-added scores. *American Journal of Education 119*(3), 445-70. https://doi.org/10.1086/669901

International Literacy Association. (2018). *Standards for the preparation of literacy professionals 2017.* Author.

Ippolito, J., & Bean, R. M. (2019). A principal's guide to supporting instructional coaching. *Educational Leadership, 77*(3), 68-73.

Kaefer, T., Neuman, S. B., & Pinkman, A. M. (2015). Pre-existing background knowledge influences socioeconomic differences in preschoolers' word learning and comprehension. *Reading Psychology, 36*(3), 203-31. https://doi:10.1080/02702711.2013.843064

Kraft, M. A., Blazar, D., & Hogan, D. (2018). The effect of teacher coaching on instruction and achievement: A meta-analysis of the causal evidence. *Review of Educational Research, 88*(4), 547-588. https://doi.org/10.3102/00346 54318759268

L'Allier, S., Elish-Piper, L., & Bean, R. M. (2010). What matters for elementary literacy coaching? Guiding principles for instructional improvement and student achievement. *The Reading Teacher, 63*(7). https://doi:10.1598/RT.63.7.2

Marzano, R. J., Frontier, T., & Livingston, D. (2011). *Effective supervision: Supporting the art and science of teaching.* Association of Supervision and Curriculum Development.

Petscher, Y., Cabell, S. Q., Catts, H. W., Compton, D. L., Foorman, B. R., Hart, S. A., ... & Wagner, R. K. (2020). How the science of reading informs 21st-century education. *Reading Research Quarterly, 55*(S1), S267-S282. https://doi:10.1002/rrq.352

Pianta, R., Kinzie, M., Justice, L., Pullen, P., Fan, X., & Lloyd, J. (2003). *Web training: Pre-K teachers, literacy, and relationships. Effectiveness of early childhood program, curricula, and interventions.* National Institute of Child Health and Human Development.

Rentfro, E. R. (2007). Professional learning communities impact student success. *Leadership Compass, 5*(2), 1-3.

Reutzel, D. R., & Fawson, P. C. (2021). Understanding literacy learning in the early years: A leader's guide. In S. B. Wepner & D. J. Quatroche (Eds.), *The administration and supervision of literacy programs* (6th ed., pp. 55–68). Teachers College Press.

Reutzel, D. R., Smith, J. A., & Fawson, P. C. (2005). An evaluation of two approaches for teaching reading comprehension strategies in the primary years using science information texts. *Early Childhood Research Quarterly, 20*(3), 276–305. https://doi.10.1016/j.ecresq.2005.07.002

Shulman, L. (1987). Knowledge and teaching: Foundations of the new reform. *Harvard Educational Review, 57*(1), 1–23.

Stoetzel, L., & Shedrow, S. J. (2021). Making the move online: Interactive read-alouds for the virtual classroom. *The Reading Teacher, 74*(6), 747–756. https://doi:10.1002/trtr.2006

Sullivan, S., & Glanz, J. (2013). *Supervision that improves teaching and learning.* Corwin.

Wexler, N. (2020). How reading instruction fails black and brown children. https://www.forbes.com/sites/nataliewexler/2020/06/06/how-reading-instruction-fails-black-and-brown-children/#fe471384ebe8

Willingham, D. T. (2017). *The reading mind: A cognitive approach to understanding how the mind reads.* Jossey-Bass.

Wohlstetter P., & Malloy, C. L. (2001). Organizing for literacy achievement: Using school governance to improve classroom practice. *Education and Urban Society, 34,* 42–65. https://doi.org/10.1177/0013124501341004

CHAPTER 10

Leadership Content Knowledge for Early Childhood

Making Feedback Meaningful

Maria Boeke Mongillo and Kristine Reed Woleck

PREFOCUS GUIDING QUESTIONS

- As you begin thinking about your understanding of early childhood teaching and learning, what do you think Sir Ken Robinson means by the following quote from his 2010 Ted Talk, "A three-year-old is not half a six-year-old"?
- When evaluating and supervising early childhood teachers, what do you believe are the most effective and important teacher and student "look-fors" when observing and offering feedback, and do they differ from those in older grades?
- What are the strengths and shortcomings of your school or district's supervision and evaluation system in providing you with tools to provide meaningful feedback to early childhood staff?

INTRODUCTION

In general, teachers of all grades and content areas are interested in receiving feedback that is timely and constructive and directly connects to their specific context. While the challenge of providing focused feedback is present for all educational leaders, it can be particularly evident for leaders of early childhood (EC) programs who work with students from birth through age eight, as there are diverse pathways to becoming an EC leader.

Some leaders may move from being EC teachers to a leadership position, having experience and knowledge of working with students but not adults, while other leaders may come through traditional educational leadership programs that address adult learning but often do not require specific experience or training in EC student needs. As a result, many EC leaders may need support in offering effective feedback to EC teachers to support both teacher and student growth.

This combines with the struggle the field of EC faces as it tries to address the physical, social, cognitive, emotional, and linguistic needs of young learners in developmentally appropriate ways while confronting the pressure of increasing academic demands on this age group.

Furthermore, while teacher evaluation and supervision systems provide a mechanism for assuring teacher quality, growth, and retention at all levels, EC teacher quality and retention are especially important because EC is a critical developmental period for children. High-quality EC programs have been shown to improve and sustain positive student outcomes, including higher scores on reading and math tests, higher attendance and lower discipline rates, and more mature social interactions and behaviors, as well as support better overall health (Bakken et al., 2017; Nores & Barnett, 2010).

These positive outcomes are more pronounced for students living in poverty, and EC education may offer protective factors to mitigate the impact of any risk factors young students may experience. In all classrooms, the teacher is the most significant influence on the caliber of classroom environment, instruction, and interactions. Thus, for leaders targeted feedback is a vehicle for providing support and fostering the growth of EC teachers as part of the mechanism for overall program and student outcome improvements.

With these ideas as the foundation, the focus of this chapter will be on some key ideas about how young children learn and the best instructional practices for supporting that learning. The chapter will provide readers the opportunity to reflect on their knowledge of young learners, consider the kinds of feedback they currently give to their EC, and expand their knowledge and understanding of EC. The goal will be to help leaders better support and develop EC teachers through actionable, appropriate, and relevant feedback, and navigate some of the tensions inherent in the evaluation and broader educational structures and systems.

BACKGROUND

Leadership content knowledge (LCK) is defined as "that knowledge of subjects and how students learn them that is used by administrators when they function as instructional leaders" (Stein & Nelson, 2003, p. 445). Leaders who develop LCK are more successful with engaging in collaborative conversations and providing specific feedback following classroom observations (Fuentes & Jimerson, 2019). Teachers are looking for feedback that is meaningful and connected to the content leaders observe, and the level to which leaders understand the content influences how well they can interact with teachers and shape instruction (Overholt & Szabocsik, 2013).

Leaders with LCK for a content area or grade level are better able to determine how to focus on both teacher and student behaviors during an observation, offer concrete suggestions for instructional improvement, support context-specific teacher growth, and better allocate resources. This may shape the written and oral feedback leaders give, as well as the structure and content of pre- and postobservation discussions and questions.

Yet many leaders, particularly principals responsible for EC education programs, find themselves working with teachers in areas of "instructional mismatch" (Fuentes & Jimmerson, 2019, p. 32) since they often have little or no training or experience with EC (Bish et al., 2011; Goncu et al., 2014; Lieberman, 2016; Mead, 2011; Shore et al., 2010). Few states require leadership preparation programs to offer specific content about or clinical experiences with EC, which may unintentionally imply that EC programmatic needs are the same as those that serve older students.

Many leaders rely on their own experience as parents or informal conversations with EC practitioners to shape their understanding of young learners, rather than engaging in systematic or formal professional learning experiences. Instructional mismatch has important implications, as leaders who are unfamiliar with young children's needs may find themselves relying on knowledge of grade levels and subject areas in which they have experience and expertise (Fuentes & Jimmerson, 2019).

This may cause leaders to make suggestions based on what is appropriate for older grades, and encourage classroom practices that may not foster the learning of young students (Goncu et al., 2014; Mead, 2011; Mongillo, 2017).

A further challenge in providing feedback to EC teachers is the tension between EC and the kindergarten-to-grade-12 public education system called "colliding worlds" (McCabe & Sipple, 2011, p. 2) as there are differences in teaching philosophies, teacher qualifications, and funding between the two. The roles and responsibilities of EC teachers often differ from that of their counterparts in other classrooms, as do their teaching and assessment methods.

Teachers in the early elementary grades, who straddle both worlds, may be particularly impacted by these pressures. EC teachers often express concern and frustration about the teacher evaluation systems, as the instruments and systems for providing EC teachers feedback are likely to be the same as those used for teachers of older students and they may conflict with EC best practices if interpreted narrowly or applied literally.

While no leader can have complete understanding of pedagogy and practices for every grade level and content area, to become effective at providing feedback to teachers that ultimately supports student learning, leaders should engage in "targeted and intentional instructional learnership" (Fuentes & Jimmerson, 2019, p. 33). In practice, instructional learnership is about strategically accessing resources and the expertise of colleagues to develop an understanding of the larger, overarching ideas related to a discipline such as EC.

Having this knowledge can assist leaders in identifying both struggling and exemplary teachers and providing all teachers with the necessary supports to grow their practice. Moreover, teachers indicate that in order for them to view the feedback they receive as credible and worth action, they need to view their leader as having appropriate knowledge of content and instruction (Liu et al., 2019). Further, LCK may also aid in a leader being able to interpret or reframe the district or school level evaluation materials used for a wide range of grade and content areas in ways that are contextually appropriate.

GUIDING PRINCIPLES OF EARLY CHILDHOOD EDUCATION

The National Association for the Education of Young Children (NAEYC) is a professional organization that offers support for EC professionals through defining quality practice, influencing policy, and conducting research. In 2020, they revised their initial 12 Principles for Developmentally Appropriate Practice (DAP) to the following 9 Principles of Child Development and Learning and Implications That Inform Practice in order to reflect current research.

In their recommendations following the presentation of the principles, NAEYC suggested the need to "support and incentivize professional development for administrators, supervisors, and those responsible for assessment and evaluation of early childhood educators to ensure they understand the principles and guidelines of developmentally appropriate practice and use them to inform decisions regarding program implementation" (p. 30). While the principles present as a linear list in table 10.1, NAEYC cautioned that the relationships among the different principles are more complex.

Though all principles are important to EC teaching and learning, a few may be worth highlighting for leaders looking to develop their LCK, as they may differ from learning practices and expectations in classrooms of older students. First, within a strong EC classroom and curriculum, there should be many opportunities for children to play, as it is the mechanism through which young children learn.

Though the EC field struggles to formally define play, there are agreed upon characteristics of play including that children enjoy play, are intrinsi-

Table 10.1. Principles of child development and learning and implications that inform practice (NAEYC, 2020)

1. Development and learning are dynamic processes that reflect the complex interplay between a child's biological characteristics and the environment, each shaping the other as well as future patterns of growth.
2. All domains of child development—physical development, cognitive development, social and emotional development, and linguistic development (including bilingual or multilingual development), as well as approaches to learning—are important; each domain both supports and is supported by the others.
3. Play promotes joyful learning that fosters self-regulation, language, cognitive and social competencies, as well as content knowledge across disciplines. Play is essential for all children, birth through age eight.
4. Although general progressions of development and learning can be identified, variations due to cultural contexts, experiences, and individual differences must also be considered.
5. Children are active learners from birth, constantly taking in and organizing information to create meaning through their relationships, their interactions with their environment, and their overall experiences.
6. Children's motivation to learn is increased when their learning environment fosters their sense of belonging, purpose, and agency. Curricula and teaching methods build on each child's assets by connecting their experiences in the school or learning environment to their home and community settings.
7. Children learn in an integrated fashion that cuts across academic disciplines or subject areas. Because the foundations of subject area knowledge are established in early childhood, educators need subject-area knowledge, an understanding of the learning progressions within each subject area, and pedagogical knowledge about teaching each subject area's content effectively.
8. Development and learning advance when children are challenged to achieve at a level just beyond their current mastery and when they have many opportunities to reflect on and practice newly acquired skills.
9. Used responsibly and intentionally, technology and interactive media can be valuable tools for supporting children's development and learning.

cally motivated to engage in play, and do so spontaneously; that the focus of play is on process rather than product; and that play is nonliteral, pretend, and driven by imagination (Johnson et al., 2012).

Play takes on many forms, including functional or practice, constructive, dramatic or symbolic, and games with rules. Adults can create the conditions and provide materials to encourage the direction and focus of play, engage with children in play by incorporating language and asking questions, and help children move toward more mature stages of play.

Another aspect is the need for children to be active learners, engaging with the environment in hands-on and meaningful ways, and physically manipulating and navigating materials, space, and personal interactions. Young children need to be able to learn using multiple modalities, which helps them to activate multiple areas of the brain and form and expand neural connections.

Offering young students a variety of learning experiences allows them to try new ways of thinking, test hypotheses, make mistakes, and find solutions (Kelly, 2001). This also supports the development of the whole child, through engaging students not only in cognitive tasks, but physical, social, and emotional ones as well.

Additionally, young children need to have a strong sense of belonging, and this includes tight connections both within and between the classroom and school, and the homes and communities where the students live. Educators need to understand the sociocultural contexts of their students. Engaging parents and other caregivers is essential as their involvement is correlated to increased vocabularies and reading achievement, positive play interactions, and attitudes toward learning in children, as well as easier school transitions, fewer grade retentions, and fewer special education placements (Goncu et al., 2014).

Finally, the interdisciplinary nature of EC requires that teachers have content and pedagogical knowledge across a range of disciplines and developmental domains. High-quality EC classrooms create learning environments that allow children to explore concepts using different disciplinary lenses, and this should be reflected within the classroom environment, instructional activities, and assessments.

Furthermore, exploration into the development of executive functioning and self-regulation found that children are not born with these skills, but with the potential to develop them beginning in EC (Center on the Developing Child, 2012). These foundational skills have lasting impacts on school achievement, positive behaviors, good health, and workplace success.

To foster the initial development of these skills, there are three critical factors:

1. *Relationships*, where children have access to adults who support and guide them toward independence, and model for and engage with them in activities that promote skill development
2. *Activities*, in which students take part in repeated practice with increasingly complex activities including play and physical exercise
3. *Places*, where students feel safe and have the space to employ creativity investigation, and physical activity

In these critical factors we again see the highlighted role of adult role models, the importance of play and physical interactions with the world, and the significance of repetition in an environment that fosters emotional safety and belonging.

EVALUATION CONSIDERATIONS

For teacher evaluation systems to be effective for both assessing teacher quality and providing feedback to support teacher growth, all tools should be aligned to disciplinary or content standards and include all domains of the standards (Martella & Connors-Tadros, 2014). However, most evaluation frameworks commonly in use have not been developed for use in EC, nor have they been tested or validated within the EC context. As a result, districts and schools who are designing systems based on these frameworks may unwittingly develop rubrics and evaluation tools or models that are inadequate for meeting EC teacher and leader needs.

The purpose of feedback in the evaluation system is to support teachers in improving classroom practices to ultimately advance student outcomes. Ideally, classroom observation feedback should motivate teachers to build content and pedagogical content knowledge, try new instructional or classroom management strategies, or seek out professional learning opportunities, though many teachers indicate the systems in place fail to do so (Liu et al., 2019).

This chapter now draws on examples from practitioner experience to share perspectives on feedback that can address specific needs of EC teachers and the way systemic tools might be leveraged for this feedback.

From the Teacher Perspective

To ensure that teachers deem leader feedback relevant and meaningful to their practice in the moment, EC leaders may want to consider some of the specific role demands and needs of EC teachers as well as the characteristics of effective early childhood settings and instruction. These can span such typical areas of supervision and evaluation systems as learning environment, instructional practices, and assessment.

Leaders will want to consider the specific implications of early childhood education relative to these areas and use this to inform the questions they pose to teachers in postobservation conferences; these questions in turn set the stage for feedback to teachers that is relevant and meets teacher needs. Table 10.2 outlines some of these look-fors in EC settings and instruction and the related observation questions that can support meaningful feedback discussions with teachers.

Regarding the learning environment, young children require space for movement, hands-on learning opportunities, and play as a vehicle for consolidating and extending ideas. This is a learning environment that is organized yet flexible. Predictability in the space, materials, and routines allows children to take cognitive risks. At the same time, there must also

Table 10.2. Characteristics of effective early childhood settings and instruction: Look-fors and observation questions to ask

Area	Look-Fors	Observation Questions
Learning environment	The classroom space, schedule, and expectations are predictable yet flexible Materials are accessible and organized for students to initiate tasks or pursue ideas Physical space and furniture allow for movement and motor breaks Flexible seating and work spaces allow for collaboration and social skills and language development Visuals, anchor charts posted are relevant and used by students Routines and transitions maximize instructional time	How do your classroom environment and materials support your student learning outcomes? How do established routines and transitions in the classroom influence student learning? How does your learning environment allow for a range of developmental levels and needs?
Instructional practices	Integrated instructional blocks make meaningful curriculum connections Instructional planning anticipates child's misconceptions based on developmental levels Differentiation attends to academic readiness as well as social-emotional needs of students Use of questioning and classroom discourse prompts cognitive conflict for students Use of manipulatives and technology is balanced, intentional, and effective Opportunities for language development occur across curriculum areas Opportunities for learning are embedded in play and collaborative experiences	What, if any, student misconceptions did you anticipate in this lesson and how did you address them? What additional opportunities and modalities will your students have to engage with this lesson content? How might your students consolidate and extend their learning in this lesson through play opportunities?
Assessment	Use of observations and interviews to assess student learning Examining qualitative student work samples as evidence of learning System to track qualitative student learning growth over time	What methods are you using to collect information about student learning during this lesson? What will success look and sound like for your students? Are there other contexts or settings in which to assess your students on this content? What is your method for tracking student progress over time, including qualitative growth?

be flexibility in these elements of the classroom to allow children to share ownership of the environment, collaborate with one another, and make connections across the curriculum. Teachers may find this balance of structure and flexibility to be a challenging one to navigate.

Essential in EC education is attention to language and social-emotional development, and the learning environment can be intentionally orchestrated to support these areas as well. Shared materials and space, as well as collaborative problem-solving experiences and play, create the conditions for students to consider multiple perspectives, navigate conflict, and advocate for self and others.

Facilitating discussions of classroom charters and prompting children to reflect on and share both their "aha" moments and their challenges in the classroom are elements of EC teachers' practice that cannot be scripted in a teacher guide but are essential to the classroom climate and development of the whole child.

With regard to instructional practices, curriculum units in elementary schools may be content driven. Early childhood teachers must consider how best to implement these units to meet the young child's developmental needs. This may entail embedding learning in play, differentiating instruction for academic readiness and social-emotional needs, and anticipating misconceptions that young children may hold. For instance, rather than worksheets, counting the balls in the outdoor play bin to be sure all were returned can build understandings of one-to-one correspondence and whether the arrangement of objects affects the count.

Even the master schedule in elementary schools, shaped by academic subjects, may be a challenge given the integrated nature of young children's learning. Teachers may need permission, feedback, and coaching to apply an EC lens to instruction. This requires thinking flexibly about instructional time in the EC classroom. As one example, rather than distinct "reading" and "writing" times in the daily schedule, EC classroom schedules may embed a more broadly defined literacy block that allows for integrated teaching, learning, and application of skills.

Assessment practices for young children are grounded in observation, not written assessments, and at times this could also entail individual interviews to allow students to actively demonstrate their skills and understanding. This can be especially time consuming and challenging with large class sizes, a particular concern of EC teachers. As these teachers consider the wealth of qualitative data they gain daily from their interactions with children in their classroom, feedback that steers toward systems to keep track of this data and ways to examine it with a focused lens can support decision making and next steps for learning.

From the Systems Perspective

Structures of educator supervision and evaluation systems designed for K–12 school districts typically include rubrics or frameworks for effective practice that are intended to provide clarity of expectations and shared language. This shared language about effective practice can be especially valuable as leaders provide feedback following observations or at growth conferences as part of the supervision and evaluation process. However, pitfalls exist if leaders utilize these tools for feedback to EC teachers without integrating LCK and teacher perspectives or areas of concern specific to EC education.

Rubrics related to instructional practices often integrate research that calls for clear student learning objectives (Marzano, 2009). This may look like learning targets posted for teachers and students to reference during a lesson, but it can be challenging to capture this with developmentally appropriate language for young students (Moss & Brookhart, 2012). When a leader observes teacher learning objectives posted in a kindergarten classroom, feedback can be critical in supporting a teacher to shift to student-centered communication of learning targets and questioning that prompts students to talk about and process their learning in their own words.

Rubrics may emphasize the integration of technology as a learning tool. However, this must also be interpreted in the context of EC classrooms. Given the developmental stages of young children, both physical manipulatives and virtual manipulatives can foster learning, but the interaction of the learners with the tools in an intentional manner is critical (Sarama & Clements, 2016).

For instance, measuring with nonstandard units requires young children to not only line up units, but to also recognize that there are to be no spaces or overlaps in the units in order to be accurate in the measurement. Self-correcting technology may not bring forward discrepancies in the measurement results to uncover this aspect of repeated units in the way that manipulating physical units may.

With both physical and virtual tools, questioning and classroom discourse, however, remains essential in calling children's attention to the conceptual understanding of unit iteration. Leaders with an EC lens can provide valuable feedback to teachers to ensure technology is used purposefully and effectively, embeds questioning to probe for student understanding, and balances student experiences with physical and virtual manipulatives.

Reviews of student growth data serve as a vehicle for feedback to teachers, and here too leaders will want to consider the specific context of EC development. This may entail looking together at artifacts of student learning with an understanding of EC development broadly and specific to literacy and numeracy content. Evidence of student learning may include such artifacts as their participation in rhyming games, running records in reading, children's drawings of science observations, and video clips of students explaining their mathematical thinking.

As an example, EC leaders might probe how teachers are monitoring students' phonological and phonemic awareness and manipulation of sounds, not rushing to assessments of letters in print. With the EC teacher, leaders can examine student growth evidence across the day, perhaps in morning meeting, shared reading, and play centers.

What are EC teachers looking and listening for when observing for phonological awareness skills? What patterns of errors do they notice? What does that mean for instruction? Such conversations in postobservation conferences allow leaders to provide feedback that deepens the EC teacher's use of observations and work samples, not test scores or written assessments, to inform instruction.

CONCLUSION

The leader's role is to connect the specific needs of the EC teacher with the tools available for feedback. Deepening their own understanding of EC development and how it intersects with the learning environment, instruction, and assessment, as described in this chapter, is therefore critical for leaders if they are to understand the needs and perspectives of EC teachers.

The leader can then use systemic tools such as effective teaching frameworks and rubrics, and the observation and evaluation process with greater specificity and relevance to provide teacher feedback. As the discourse and dialogue between a leader and an EC teacher is strengthened, so is the collaborative relationship.

This chapter provided leaders with insights into the specific challenges of EC teachers, particularly as their practice unfolds in K–12 settings, and offered examples of ways that tools in teacher evaluation systems can be leveraged to provide meaningful feedback to these teachers. This calls for ongoing collaboration between leaders and EC teachers, with time spent in EC classrooms, to articulate together what effective teaching and learning looks and sounds like in the EC classroom. This in turn can build capacity within the school for ongoing professional learning conversations and inquiry, repositioning feedback from evaluative to growth inducing.

POSTREADING REFLECTIONS/ACTIVITIES

- Think about the feedback you currently give to your EC teachers. How focused is it on the specific needs of EC teachers and students? What

informs your specific EC feedback and the questions you ask of a teacher during pre- and postobservation discussions?
- Review the evaluation rubric and/or system used in your school or district to record classroom observation data and provide feedback to teachers.
  - Given the information discussed in this chapter, are there specific criteria that need to be evaluated differently or through a different lens for EC teachers? If so, which criteria?
  - Of the criteria you selected, which do you feel you have the knowledge and expertise to interpret and effectively evaluate for EC teachers? For which do you need to develop a deeper understanding?

REFERENCES

Bakken, L., Brown, N., & Downing, B. (2017). Early childhood education: The long-term benefits. *Journal of Research in Childhood Education. 31*(2), 255–69. https://doi.org/10.1080/02568543.2016.1273285

Bish, M., Shore, R., & Shue, P. (2011). Preparing elementary principals for preschool. *Principal, 90*(5), 20–24. https://www.naesp.org/principal-mayjune-2011-early-childhood/principal-mayjune-2011-early-childhood

Center on the Developing Child. (2012). *Executive Function* (InBrief). www.developingchild.harvard.edu

Fuentes, S. Q., & Jimerson, J. B. (2019). Tackling instructional mismatch: Targeted, intentional learning can build leaders' content knowledge. *The Learning Professional, 40*(5), 32–35. https://learningforward.org/journal/resilient-leadership/tackling-instructional-mismatch/

Goncu, A., Main, C., Perone, A., & Tozer, S. (2014). Crossing the boundaries: The need to integrate school leadership and early childhood education. *Mid-Western Educational Researcher, 26*(1), 66–75. http://www.mwera.org/MWER/volumes/v26/issue1/v26n1-Goncu-Main-Perone-Tozer-POLICY-BRIEFS.pdf

Johnson, J. E., Sevimli-Celik, S., & Al-Mansour, M. (2012). Play in early childhood education. In O. N. Saracho & B. Spodek (Eds.), *Handbook of research on the education of young children* (3rd ed., pp. 265–74). Routledge.

Kelly, M. (Ed.) (2001). Active learning in the classroom: Common understandings. In *The primary program: Growing and learning in the heartland* (2nd ed., pp. 151–64). Office of Children and Families, Nebraska Department of Education.

Lieberman, A. (2016). *Leading for the early years: Principals' reflections on the need for better preparation.* New America. https://static.newamerica.org/attachments/13105-principals-corner/5.4Early-Ed-Principal-5.509c74b6308a4559aad9bbfd57e3a472.pdf

Liu, Y., Visone, J. D., Mongillo, M. B., & Lisi, P. (2019). What matters to teachers if evaluation is meant to help them improve? *Studies in Educational Evaluation, 61,* 45–54. https://doi.org/10.1016/j.stueduc.2019.01.006

Martella, J., & Connors-Tadros, L. (2014). *Evaluating early childhood educators prekindergarten through third grade: Supplement to the practical guide to designing com-*

prehensive educator evaluation systems. American Institutes for Research. https://gtlcenter.org/sites/default/files/Early_Childhood_Supplement.pdf

Marzano, R. J. (2009). *Designing and teaching learning goals and objectives*. Marzano Research Laboratory.

McCabe, L. A., & Sipple, J. W. (2011). Colliding worlds: Practical and political tensions of prekindergarten implementation in public schools. *Educational Policy, 25*(1), e1–e26. https://doi.org/10.1177/0895904810387415

Mead, S. (2011). *Prek–3rd: Principals as crucial instructional leaders* (PreK–3rd Policy to Action Brief No. Seven). Foundation for Child Development. http://fcd-us.org/sites/default/files/FCD%20PrincipalsBrief7.pdf

Mongillo, M. B. (2017). Preparing school leaders for young learners in the United States. *Global Education Review, 4*(3), 37–55. https://files.eric.ed.gov/fulltext/EJ1158197.pdf

Moss, C. M., & Brookhart, S. M. (2012). *Learning targets: Helping students aim for understanding in today's lesson*. ASCD.

National Association for the Education of Young Children. (2020). *Developmentally Appropriate Practice: A Position Statement of the National Association for the Education of Young Children*. https://www.naeyc.org/resources/position-statements/dap/contents

Nores, M., & Barnett, W. S. (2010). Benefits of early childhood interventions across the world: (Under) investing in the very young. *Economics of Education Review, 29*, 271–82. https://doi.org/10.1016/j.econedurev.2009.09.001

Overholt, R., & Szabocsik, S. (2013). Leadership content knowledge for literacy: Connecting literacy teachers and their principals. *The Clearing House, 86*, 53–58. https://doi.org/10.1080/00098655.2012.742034

Sarama, J., & Clements, D. H. (2016). Physical and virtual manipulatives: What is "concrete"? In P. S. Moyer-Packenham (Ed.), *International perspectives on teaching and learning mathematics with virtual manipulatives* (pp. 71–93). Springer International Publishing. https://doi.org/10.1007/978-3-319-32718-1_4

Shore, R. A., Shue, P. L., & Lambert, R. G. (2010). Ready or not, here come the pre-schoolers! *Phi Delta Kappan 92*(3), 32–34. http://dx.doi.org/10.1177/003172171009200309

Stein, M. K., & Nelson, B. S. (2003). Leadership content knowledge. *Educational Evaluation and Policy Analysis, 25*(4), 423–48. https://doi.org/10.3102/01623737025004423

CHAPTER 11

Supervision and Observation in the Gifted Education Classroom

Keri M. Guilbault, Kimberley L. Chandler, and Sarah A. Caroleo

PREFOCUS GUIDING QUESTIONS

- What are the best practices in teaching and learning related to gifted and talented education?
- What are the roles of building principals and other instructional leaders relative to supervising teachers involved in gifted education?
- What are key strategies and teaching behaviors to look for in a gifted and talented classroom?

INTRODUCTION

In this chapter, the prefocus guiding questions serve as a backdrop for information about processes of supervision in gifted and talented education. Given that this content may be new to administrators, a definition of gifted learners and an overview of best practices in gifted education are provided. Having at least a fundamental understanding of these practices is important for anyone who may be involved in the supervision of teachers of the gifted.

A key component of this section is helping the reader to understand how the teaching behaviors and classroom environment in a gifted and talented setting should differ from those found in the general education classroom. This includes information about professional standards that guide practices in gifted education.

The second portion of the chapter provides practical applications of the information for those involved in supervising teachers in gifted education settings. Although central office gifted education coordinators may participate in the observation of teachers of the gifted, principals are often the ones responsible for the evaluation of special programs personnel assigned to their buildings; thus, this chapter is aimed primarily at the principal audience. Information is included about how to conduct observations and feedback in a gifted education setting, as well as how to distinguish elements that differ from what is done in a general education setting.

DEFINITION OF GIFTED LEARNERS

Gifted learners are a category of students that perform or have the ability to perform at remarkably higher levels "compared to other students of the same age, experience, and environment in one or more domains" (National Association for Gifted Children, 2019, p. 1). These students come from all backgrounds and are present in every school. There is no federal mandate to identify or serve students with gifts and talents; states have the authority to set their own definition of giftedness, processes, and criteria for determining eligibility, funding, and teacher credentials.

As of 2019, approximately 38 states require formal identification of students with gifts and talents. Data collected during the 2018–2019 academic year from a national survey revealed 21 states provide dedicated funding for gifted education to their local education agencies (LEAs) in amounts ranging from $237,200 (Wisconsin) to $428,288,310 (Texas) (Rinn et al., 2020). Only 26 states require teachers of the gifted to hold a gifted endorsement or gifted and talented certification.

To find information about specific state policies and definitions of gifted and talented, visit the NAGC State of the States website (https://nagc.org/state-of-states). Regardless of how they are defined, or if they are formally identified in the local school system, all teachers and administrators should have some basic knowledge about how to meet the needs of these students in the classroom.

BEST PRACTICES IN GIFTED EDUCATION

Students with gifts and talents hold distinct cognitive, social, and emotional characteristics and needs and, therefore, require certain forms of instruction to healthfully develop their potential. Using a large body of gifted education literature to guide their work, the National Association for Gifted Children (NAGC) developed a set of evidence-based standards for teaching, learning, and programming, which outline how educators and districts should establish and sustain these responsive environments (Corwith et al., 2019). These standards are synthesized below.

Teaching Practices

Teachers should know and understand cognitive and affective characteristics associated with giftedness, as well as how these traits may develop differently over time and across individuals from all linguistic, racial, cultural, socioeconomic, and ability backgrounds (Mathies et al., 2018). With this knowledge, they can identify students' academic and social-emotional needs and guide them in their understanding of their own interests and strengths.

Teachers of the gifted should model metacognitive strategies (like goal setting, self-assessment, and self-monitoring) and cognitive strategies (like organization, rehearsal, and elaboration) and embed opportunities to practice those strategies into their lessons (VanTassel-Baska et al., 2009). They should also provide time for gifted learners to reflect on their preferred learning strategies, identify their biases, and acknowledge how their identities, cultures, and values shape their behavior and learning.

Journaling and group discussions are meaningful tools to facilitate this. Attentive teachers of the gifted not only guide their students in these self-discovery processes but also learn their students' passions so that they can refer them to opportunities to deepen their knowledge and skills, such as mentorships, apprenticeships, and extracurricular enrichment classes.

For instructional planning, effective teachers of the gifted use frequent and varied assessments to gauge students' content proficiency and levels of readiness (which is the current combination of background knowledge, skills, and dispositions with which they enter a learning task) (Tomlinson, 2015). If students have already grasped a standard or concept, their teacher should be prepared to compact, deepen, or accelerate instruction according to their needs; if they have not, the teacher similarly must be prepared to frontload the prerequisite vocabulary or background knowledge for the lesson or unit.

Formative assessments like pretests and exit tickets provide teachers with information about students' current levels of proficiency, and they can use the results to inform their instruction for the following lesson or unit. Product-based and performance-based assessments, as well as personal portfolios, supply holistic evaluations of gifted students' learning and socio-emotional progress, which can be shared with the student's guardians and classroom teachers for maximum support (VanTassel-Baska, 2005).

When teachers of the gifted observe academic concerns or notice patterns of underachievement (which occurs when a student performs below the levels with which they are capable), they can responsibly address student needs and provide targeted interventions of support. They can also use assessments to provide feedback which offers encouragement as well as opportunities to promote persistence. In feedback, teachers of the gifted should primarily focus on students' effort, while conveying their high expectations and reframing mistakes as opportunities for growth.

Learning Processes

Students with gifts and talents require learning processes that are planned and facilitated in line with their levels of readiness, areas of strength, and personal interests (Rogers, 2007). Instruction should primarily stem from or align with state standards; however, instead of using typical grade-level curriculum, teachers of the gifted should either deepen, expand, or accelerate content for students who have mastered the standards.

Gifted learners often benefit from instruction organized through broad concepts and themes, which require inquiry and critical thinking, as opposed to rote memorization of facts. Ideally, teachers should incorporate students' strengths and interests into learning to motivate them and foster their talent.

Learning should be balanced, meaning that students receive opportunities to work alone, collaborate with like-minded peers, and learn alongside age-level peers; gifted learners should not primarily function as a tutor to classmates. They especially thrive when learning is connected to real-world or authentic problems, so experiential or service learning is optimal (Stephens et al., 2016).

High-ability gifted students learn particularly well through acceleration options, like grade skipping, subject skipping, content/unit acceleration, or curriculum compacting; the form of acceleration should match the child's current level of strength and need (Assouline et al., 2015). If teachers observe repeated advanced performance within a child, they can advocate for acceleration and collaborate with the family and school stakeholders to enact it using research-based tools such as the *Iowa Acceleration Scale*, 3rd edition (Assouline et al., 2009).

When formal acceleration is not appropriate, differentiated learning can provide a flexible means to study advanced content. Teachers who differentiate adapt students' learning processes through the content they study, the process in which they learn, and the product(s) they create. To do this, they should use flexible grouping informed by pre- and postassessment results, so students experience learning fit to their current level of development. No matter students' prescribed levels, high-quality curriculum should be used.

Gifted learners also benefit from enrichment opportunities which expose them to a variety of disciplines and content beyond the grade-level curriculum. If teachers supply enrichment, they should infuse problem-solving, higher-level thinking, complexity, and use of various technologies into learning.

Since gifted learners may experience unique social-emotional processes (such as overexcitabilities, perfectionism, and underachievement), they thrive in learning environments that supply affective instruction aligned with their needs (Hébert, 2010). Bibliotherapy is a process in which students read a shared text with a protagonist that experiences similar socio-emotional challenges, and in guided reading groups, students discuss the character's coping skills and reflect on how they relate to them (Halsted, 2009).

This can be a particularly effective strategy for gifted students of color and those from traditionally underrepresented groups in advanced learning programs (Ford et al., 2019).

Character education embedded into the curriculum provides an opportunity to develop affective skills like leadership, respect, and empathy. Teachers can have gifted students consider their strengths and limitations, set goals, practice perspective-taking, journal, and role play problem-solving and conflict resolution. They can also introduce students to academic, artistic, or creative competitions which allow them to practice their leadership skills.

Program Models

Programs for gifted learners can take on different forms, depending on state and district policies. Magnet schools, self-contained gifted classes, or special classes like honors, AP, or dual enrollment are often facilitated through full-time homogeneous groups (Rimm et al., 2018). Full-time heterogeneous programs consist of cluster grouping (where groups of four to six gifted students are placed in an otherwise heterogeneous classroom) and differentiation in a grade-level classroom. In these full-time programs, the extent of gifted education services relies primarily on the classroom teachers' skills and delivery of instruction.

Several part-time programs exist, such as pull-out enrichment classes, push-in services (where a gifted specialist provides instruction to gifted students in the grade-level classroom), consultation (where a gifted specialist meets regularly with classroom teachers who work directly with gifted students to advise and support them in their instructional planning) and leveled instructional groups for certain subjects. These programs are often led by a distinct teacher of the gifted, although classroom teachers may facilitate leveled groups in the classroom.

In some cases, teachers of the gifted may be responsible to oversee students' acceleration services or connect them with enrichment opportunities that extend their learning. No matter the program model, the teacher of the gifted should coordinate their instruction and services with the students' classroom teachers to compliment, extend, and enrich instruction.

Principals may prioritize the development of distinct teacher skills and competencies based on their district or school-based delivery model, as illustrated in table 11.1. The NAGC has developed free resources and tools for administrators that may be helpful for program planning and evaluation. (See the NAGC Administrator Toolbox: http://www.nagc.org/resources-publications/resources-administrators/administrator-toolbox.)

Table 11.1. Observable strategies based on service delivery model

Gifted Service Delivery Model	What to Look For
Pull-out resource class	Extension activities connected to the general curriculum, process skill development, affective curriculum, communication with classroom teacher
Honors, AP, IB	Faster pace, above-level materials, authentic problem- or project-based learning activities
Co-teaching with inclusion	Collaboration, modeling of extended or creative teacher questioning, social-emotional strategies
Self-contained gifted classroom	Above-grade level materials, learning opportunities tied to students' interests and strengths, affective curriculum
Cluster grouping	Formative assessments, differentiation, above-level materials, management of various groups
Consultation	Collaboration, coaching, knowledge of and access to a variety of gifted education content materials and resources

THE ROLE OF SUPERVISION IN GIFTED EDUCATION

The role of supervision in gifted education could be considered to have two purposes. The first purpose is using supervision as a means to determine the nature of the interactions between teachers and students in the teaching and learning process. The second purpose is employing supervision as a means to ensure that gifted students' needs are met. Understanding these purposes and the relationship between them is important for anyone who supervises teachers of gifted students.

Using supervision as a way to determine the nature of the interactions between teachers and students in the teaching and learning process is a fundamental part of the continuous improvement cycle in any educational setting. "For continuous improvement of this interaction within a classroom, educators and administrators need to employ accurate assessments of instruction measured against clear standards, which must be aligned with effective practices" (Farah & Chandler, 2018, p. 276).

In the case of supervision in a gifted education classroom, this implies that the supervisor should have at least a general knowledge of the relevant, evidence-based standards and should use reliable and valid instruments for observations. Understanding the teaching practices, learning processes, and program models typically employed in gifted education is essential.

The administrator must be able to distinguish the elements that differ from what would be present in a general education setting. In order to provide the type of feedback that promotes continuous improvement, a principal should be conversant with expectations about teaching and learning in this special context.

The second and closely related purpose of supervision in the gifted education classroom is ensuring that gifted students' needs are met. Principals can determine the degree of alignment of teachers' instructional methods to best practices in gifted education by using structured observation practices and instruments tailored to the gifted education setting (Peters & Gates, 2010).

Doing so provides administrators with key information about the strengths and weaknesses of a given teacher's pedagogical skills. An important outcome of the analysis of this information is being able to decide the extent to which teachers are effective in meeting gifted students' instructional needs.

There are many pragmatic elements of supervision, such as conducting observations and evaluating teachers, which address district and state requirements. Ultimately, these elements aim to ensure that gifted students' needs are appropriately met. An example is the recommended teaching practice of using varied assessments to gauge content proficiency and readiness.

While this practice is promoted for all types of classrooms, the principal should understand the especially important role of assessments in the gifted education classroom for informing instructional practices related to differentiation. Following an observation in which exit tickets are used, the principal should ask about next steps to ensure appropriate differentiation.

Most teachers in gifted and talented education work in isolation in their schools with no colleagues also working specifically with this student population. Although a district gifted education coordinator may visit occasionally, building administrators are typically the individuals charged with supervising the teachers. Therefore, it is crucial for them to understand their role in supervision of teachers of the gifted and how it relates to the bigger picture of addressing diverse student needs.

Ideally, several practices should be in place in order to facilitate building administrators' work in this area. First, the district gifted education coordinator should provide all building administrators with basic training about the nature and needs of gifted students and the related implications for curriculum and instruction. Second, the district coordinator or a designee should work closely with each building administrator to help them understand how to use the district observation protocols specifically with teachers of the gifted. A third action is to establish a Professional Learning Network (PLN) with principals to assist with their continued growth.

Areas for emphasis should include understanding gifted students' development and how teachers' knowledge of this information translates into sound classroom practices. Especially important would be helping building administrators learn how to provide relevant feedback to teachers of the gifted and where to direct them for additional support.

It may also be helpful to establish a PLN for teachers of the gifted in a district as a means of providing this support. Guided by the district gifted education coordinator or a designee, the PLN could meet in person or virtually as a mechanism for professional learning. Depending on the needs of the group, topics for discussion could include curriculum differentiation, instructional resources, and lesson planning.

This network could also serve as a forum for receiving information about how they may use feedback from observations to grow and improve in their professional practice. If there are not enough teachers of the gifted in the district to form a PLN, principals can encourage them to network with state or national organizations such as the NAGC (www.nagc.org) and Supporting the Emotional Needs of the Gifted (SENG) (www.sengifted.org).

OBSERVATION AND FEEDBACK IN A GIFTED EDUCATION CLASSROOM

Observation is a complicated task. Given the fact that most school leaders have had little to no training in gifted education (Rinn et al., 2020), this process may seem even more challenging when observing a teacher of the gifted. Providing accurate and constructive feedback to teachers working with gifted students and to gifted gifted education specialists is essential to ensure high-quality instruction. Skilled principals and instructional leaders are able to adapt and use a variety of tools to guide teachers in honing their craft. Several steps are needed in this process:

- developing observer knowledge of basic gifted education pedagogy
- using common language associated with the discipline
- training observers to recognize best practices for gifted instruction
- understanding how to use required or supplemental observation tools
- collecting objective evidence from lesson observations that is free from bias
- interpreting data and observation notes to provide effective feedback and coaching

In this section, strategies, and teaching behaviors to look for in a gifted education classroom will be discussed and resources for principals and instructional leaders will be provided.

Gifted Education Observation Tools

How can a principal or instructional leader know if what they observe in a classroom aligns with gifted education pedagogy? On one hand, many best practices that stemmed from gifted education, such as differentiated instruction, higher order questioning, problem-based learning, and student-centered learning, are indeed good practices for all learners. What is different for gifted learners, though, is that these strategies are needed earlier, and with greater frequency and intensity. Gifted students are often ready for more advanced material than is typically presented in a grade-level classroom and acquire new knowledge quickly.

When thinking about students with gifts and talents, it is important to understand that what is considered developmentally appropriate for other students at the same age may not be developmentally appropriate for the gifted student. Many gifted learners are capable of working two, three, four, or more years above grade level in one or more content areas and learn new material faster than other students (Makel et al., 2016). They are more likely to *mislearn* information when there is too much repetition; therefore, they need curriculum compacting and instruction at an accelerated pace (Assouline et al., 2015).

Take for instance, an elementary classroom in which the teacher guides students with an *I do, we do, you do* lesson format. For the advanced learner who only needs to see or hear something once, this can shut down their learning and engagement. Instead, the teacher can modify the lesson by guiding gifted learners to develop critical thinking through advanced questioning techniques such as Socratic inquiry.

Observers should look for instruction that adjusts to gifted learners' rate of learning, need for depth and acceleration, and personal interests. Instead of an emphasis on direct instruction, a student-centered classroom where the teacher serves as a facilitator of knowledge, encouraging deep thinking, metacognition, and collaboration, is preferred.

District-approved teacher observation scales and evaluation rubrics define criteria and performance levels but do not always fit well for use with resource teacher positions like a gifted education specialist. Besides using these required instruments, principals may refer to tools and resources that have been created specifically for use in gifted education classrooms. These provide examples of what to look for, common language, and criteria that indicate the use of research-based best practices. See table 11.2 for a list of observation forms that are available for different gifted education service delivery models.

During a preobservation conference, principals should communicate with the teacher of the gifted to select a focus area for the observation. This may be content specific (lessons that are aligned to standards) or process specific (e.g., creative thinking, problem solving, research skills, or communication). Next, they can select an appropriate supplemental tool that will help record relevant data during the observation. Selecting a tool that aligns with and complements district-approved observation forms allows the observer to provide meaningful, actionable feedback that reflects the unique role of the teacher of the gifted.

Table 11.2. Gifted education teacher observation forms

Tool	Items Observed	Program Model	Author, Year
Assessing Classroom Differentiation Protocol–Revised	Levels of engagement, pace, cognitive activity, learning director, classroom management	Mixed-ability or inclusion classroom	National Association for Gifted Children, 2009
The Differentiated Classroom Observation Scale	Pedagogy, student engagement, instructional activity, level of cognitive activity, learning director	Cluster grouped classroom, mixed-ability or inclusion classroom	Cassady et al., 2004
Purdue University Gifted Education Resource Institute Teacher Observation Form–Revised	Pedagogy, content coverage, clarity, motivational techniques, student choice, higher level thinking skills, use of technology	Enrichment program, special class, self-contained class, pull-out model	Peters & Gates, 2010
William and Mary Classroom Observation Scales, Revised	Curriculum planning and delivery, differentiation, problem solving, critical and creative thinking, research strategies, student engagement	Mixed-ability or inclusion classroom, self-contained class, cluster grouped classroom, pull-out model	VanTassel-Baska et al., 2003

In addition to these gifted education teacher observation forms, the national standards that guide gifted education programming are a useful resource. The *2019 Pre-K–Grade 12 Gifted Programming Standards* (Corwith et al., 2019) can be downloaded for free at the NAGC website (www.nacg.org). These six standards are supported by research and include evidence-based practices. The NAGC standards also align closely with commonly used teacher evaluation forms such as those by Marzano and the Danielson Framework.

Teaching Behaviors to Look for in a Gifted Education Classroom

What behaviors (and evidence of their effectiveness) should a principal look for when observing a teacher of the gifted? National standards in gifted education, national standards in subject areas, district-approved standards, student data, and district observation tools are all sources that can be used to determine what teaching behaviors to look for during an observation, and to evaluate the effectiveness of teaching strategies.

Another consideration is the school or district gifted education service delivery model. An observer will look for different teaching behaviors in a mixed ability classroom with a cluster group of four to six identified gifted students than when observing a fourth-grade, self-contained, homogeneous gifted education classroom.

Observations may be enhanced with teacher reflections. Reflections create buy-in, which empowers teachers to take charge of their own professional growth (Slade, 2018). Feedback on reflections of instructional planning and delivery leads to a deeper understanding of personal strengths and areas for professional learning. Questions that can be used to guide feedback are as follows:

- How do you use preassessment data to inform in person or virtual instruction?
- How do you develop an inclusive classroom culture that respects diversity?
- How do you motivate advanced students to reach their potential?
- In what ways do you match rigor and pace to individual learner ability?

These reflection prompts can be used to coach teachers of the gifted as they reflect on their teaching and identify areas for improvement. This may be conducted during the postobservation conference, in small teams, in professional learning communities, in discussion groups held online in the learning management system (LMS), at a faculty meeting, or written by the teacher and kept in a professional portfolio.

CONCLUSION

Because students with gifts and talents require specific learning processes and environments to succeed both academically and socioemotionally, it is imperative that those teaching them provide research-based services aligned with individual learners' strengths and needs. Understanding how gifted education best practices align with school-based program models and knowing meaningful ways to use various observation forms will support principals as they strive to ensure effective classroom instruction and achievement for *all* students.

POSTREADING REFLECTIONS/ACTIVITIES

- How might a principal use existing gifted education observation instruments to better understand desired teacher and learner behaviors for a gifted education classroom?
- Describe two resources that a principal, who is new to gifted education, could refer to for a basic orientation?
- Based on the gifted education service delivery model used in your school/district, what are three teaching strategies a principal should expect to observe? How are these different from a general education classroom?

REFERENCES

Assouline, S. G., Colangelo, N., Lupkowski-Shoplik, A., Lipscomb, J., & Forstadt, L. (2009). *Iowa acceleration scale manual: A guide for whole grade acceleration K–8* (3rd ed.). Great Potential Press.

Assouline, S., Colangelo, N., VanTassel-Baska, J., & Lupkowski-Shoplik, A. (Eds.). (2015). *A nation empowered: Evidence trumps the excuses that hold back America's brightest students* (Vols. 1 & 2). University of Iowa, The Connie Belin & Jacqueline N. Blank International Center for Gifted Education and Talent Development.

Cassady, J. C., Speirs-Neumeister, K. L., Adams, C. M., Cross, T. L., Dixon, F. A., & Pierce, R. L. (2004). The differentiated classroom observation scale. *Roeper Review, 26*, 139–46. https://doi.org/10.1080/02783190409554259

Corwith, S., Johnson, S., Lee, C., Cotabish, A., Dailey, D., & Guilbault, K. (2019). *2019 pre-k-grade 12 gifted programming standards*. Professional Standards Committee, National Association for Gifted Children. https://www.nagc.org/sites/default/files/standards/Intro%202019%20Programming%20Standards%281%29.pdf

Farah, Y. N., & Chandler, K. L. (2018). Structured observation instruments assessing instructional practices with gifted and talented students: A review of the literature. *Gifted Child Quarterly, 62*(3), 276–88. https://doi.org/10.1177/0016986218758439

Ford, D. Y., Walters, N. M., Byrd, J. A., & Harris, B. N. (2019). I want to read about me: Engaging and empowering gifted Black girls using multicultural literature and bibliotherapy. *Gifted Child Today, 42*(1), 53–57. https://doi.org/10.1177/1076217518804851

Halsted, J. W. (2009). *Some of my best friends are books: Guiding gifted readers* (2nd ed.). Great Potential Press.

Hébert, T. P. (2010). Lessons learned from my students: The impact of SEM teaching and learning on affective development. *Gifted Education International, 26*, 271–84. https://doi.org/10.1177/026142941002600313

Makel, M. C., Matthews, M. S., Peters, S. J., Rambo-Hernandez, K., & Plucker, J. A. (2016). *How can so many students be invisible? Large percentages of American students perform above grade level*. Institute for Education Policy, Johns Hopkins University School of Education.

Mathies, S., Kronborg, L., Schmitt, M., & Preckel, F. (2018). Threat or challenge? Teacher beliefs about gifted students and their relationship to teacher motivation. *Gifted and Talented International, 32*(2), 134–60. https://doi.org/10.1080/153322 76.2018.1537685

National Association for Gifted Children. (2009). *Assessing classroom differentiation protocol.* http://www.nagc.org/sites/default/files/administrators/Assessing%20Dif ferentiation%20Protocol.pdf

National Association for Gifted Children. (2019). *A definition of giftedness that guides best practice.* https://files.eric.ed.gov/fulltext/ED600145.pdf

Peters, S. J., & Gates, J. C. (2010). The teacher observation form: Revisions and updates. *Gifted Child Quarterly, 54*(3), 179–88. https://doi.org/10.1177/0016986210369258

Rimm, S. B., Siegle, D., & Davis, G. A. (2018). *Education of the gifted and talented* (7th ed.). Pearson.

Rinn, A., Mun, R. U., & Hodges, J. (2020). *2018-2019 State of the states in gifted education.* National Association for Gifted Children and the Council of State Directors of Programs for the Gifted. https://www.nagc.org/2018-2019-state-states-gifted -education

Rogers, K. B. (2007). Lessons learned about educating the gifted and talented: A synthesis of research on educational practice. *Gifted Child Quarterly, 51*(4), 382–96. https://doi.org/10.1177/0016986207306324

Slade, M. (2018). Reflection as an essential practice in professional learning for gifted education. In A. Novak & C. Weber (Eds.), *Best practices in professional learning and teacher preparation* (Vol. 1, pp. 39–50). Prufrock Press.

Stephens, K. R., Malone, D., & Griffith, A. P. (2016). Service-learning in gifted education: Addressing cognitive and affective domains. In K. R. Stephens & F. A. Karnes (Eds.), *Introduction to curriculum design in gifted education* (pp. 281–305). Routledge.

Tomlinson, C. A. (2015). Teaching for excellence in academically diverse classrooms. *Society, 52*, 203–9. https://doi.org/10.1007/s12115-015-9888-0

VanTassel-Baska, J. (2005). Gifted programs and services: What are the nonnegotiables? *Theory into Practice, 44*(2), 90–97. https://doi.org/10.1207/s15430421 tip4402_3

VanTassel-Baska, J., Avery, L., Struck, J., Feng, A., Bracken, B., Drummond, D., & Stambaugh, T. (2003). *The William and Mary classroom observation scales–revised (COS-R).* William and Mary Center for Gifted Education.

VanTassel-Baska, J., Bracken, B., Feng, A., & Brown, E. (2009). A longitudinal study of enhancing critical thinking and reading comprehension in Title I classrooms. *Journal for the Education of the Gifted, 33*(1), 7–37. https://doi.org /10.1177/016235320903300102

CHAPTER 12

The Value and Necessity of Differentiation in Observation and Feedback for Career and Technical Education Teachers

Lee Westberry and Sonya Addison-Stewart

PREFOCUS GUIDING QUESTIONS

- How are career and technical education (CTE) observations different than traditional classroom observations?
- What considerations should be given when providing feedback for CTE teachers?
- How can you help CTE teachers develop and grow beyond their content knowledge?

INTRODUCTION

Career and technical education (CTE) has drastically changed over the past 20 years. CTE programs in schools not only provide students with academic and technical skills but also the knowledge and training needed in specified careers. For example, automotive technology, advanced manufacturing, and health sciences are considered CTE programs.

Not only have CTE teachers been charged with educating a more diverse population with different needs and abilities, but CTE courses have morphed into a combination of academic and technical expertise. Now with the advent of college and career readiness academic standards, college and career pathways are not always considered separate entities (Saeger, 2017), and the negative stigma associated with technical education is changing (Cheng & Hitt, 2018; Westberry, 2001).

In fact, studies suggest that students who earn CTE certifications experience higher graduation rates and higher earning potentials (Durham & Bragg, 2019), a correlation that was reserved for college graduates in the past. Furthermore, CTE programs can also help to narrow the equity gaps for traditionally marginalized populations in that minority students, while in high school, can earn national certifications and dual credit with institutions of higher education (Rosen et al., 2018).

This chapter will explore the differences between CTE classrooms and traditional academic classroom expectations, to include the use of modeling, teaming, peer-to-peer learning, safety protocols, twenty-first-century soft skills, and performance assessments. Unfortunately, most teacher evaluation instruments do not consider these differences and do not provide for variances in the different settings.

THE CTE TEACHER

With a new industry and governmental foci on career readiness, CTE programs are earning more attention. However, this attention must not become a hindrance to properly staffing and supporting CTE programs and instructors. Support for these CTE teachers is critical, as the national teacher shortage is not limited to academic areas alone (Fletcher, 2018). With teacher shortages showing no abatement any time soon, administrators must consider the needs of CTE teachers and pay special attention to support systems if teacher retention is a priority.

Typically, CTE teachers transition to education from industry. With increased industry recruitment efforts due to the shortage of workers today, this support becomes even more crucial in an effort to retain teachers. A 2021 Korn Ferry (2022) survey revealed that 55 percent of respondents believe that employee turnover will increase in 2022. A large majority (74 percent) of companies responded that companies suffer a shortage of skills and capabilities needed for the future. These statistics can translate to even higher teacher turnover in CTE, as these teachers may leave the field for more pay in industry.

Because of the many differences that exist between a traditional academic class and a CTE classroom, administrators must consider these variances when providing support through observations and feedback—instructional supervision. Some similarities in classrooms will exist, such as the need for direct instruction and modeling.

However, CTE classrooms should mimic the workplace in which students are utilizing a more hands-on approach to learning, as standards for CTE programs are skills based, not content based. Research does exist on the need for the professional learning of CTE teachers (Bradley, 2014; Sturko & Gregson, 2008); however, a paucity of research exists on quality feedback for CTE teachers.

In addition, CTE instructors themselves must be considered in the process. Most CTE instructors have valuable industry experience that must transfer to classroom instruction. However, these same instructors may not have experienced the traditional teacher education pathway for certification. As a result, the varied experiences and preparation for teaching can directly impact classroom experiences for students and teachers. Understanding the lack of training is pivotal in providing support for CTE teachers as more support is often needed.

UNDERSTANDING THE CTE CLASSROOM

As industries evolve, become obsolete, or even develop, CTE teachers are faced with the challenge of the best ways to prepare the youth for work and workplace expectations. The acquisition of technical skills is certainly on the forefront of teachers' minds, but that is not all. Teachers are also charged with teaching twenty-first-century workforce skills that transcend industries and are valued in all workplaces. These skills include the hard and soft skills identified by industry, as technical skills alone will not ensure success (Lazarus, 2013).

Because CTE classrooms are to mimic the workplace to prepare students adequately for next steps, these 21st Century Skills should be apparent in the instruction and opportunities provided to students: problem solving, collaboration, critical thinking, and communication (Care et al., 2018). The National Board for Professional Teaching Standards (2014) state,

> Accomplished teachers align curricula with students' needs and modify them consistently to meet the changing demands of the labor market. This type of ongoing evaluation and revision allows teachers to connect the emerging talents and abilities of their students with clearly articulated requirements of business and industry. The CTE learning environment is centered on student needs and academic preparation, all pointing toward the goal of acquiring workplace values, developing life skills, and realizing professional aspirations. (p. 23)

The juxtaposition lies in the evaluation of teachers, which largely focuses on knowledge-based approaches; whereas, CTE teachers should be evaluated on both content knowledge and skill development as well as 21st Century Skills development to help ensure future employment success. These 21st-century learning skills are often referred to as the 4 C's: communication, collaboration, critical thinking, and creativity (Partnership for 21st Century Skills, 2009). These skills should be readily apparent in instruction, and students should be taught how to navigate these skills through mentoring, peer-to-peer instruction, and teaming.

Many CTE classrooms have a traditional classroom space for direct instruction as well as a lab space. While some may only have a classroom space, such as computer programming, others may only have a lab space, such as horticulture or cosmetology. Observations, depending on the timing, may occur strictly in one space or the other (classroom or lab). The teacher behaviors in the different spaces may be just as different as the spaces themselves. The spaces will vary as much as the programs do, and teacher behaviors will vary depending on the space provided.

There is not a one size fits all CTE classroom. However, what should not vary is that a CTE classroom should be filled with hands-on, active learning at all times. A computer programming class, which is part of CTE, will provide some direct instruction and modeling, but students will work primarily on the programming itself. Hopefully, students are collaborative and solving problems in the code among groups, which is a direct reflection of the industry.

Welding students may only receive instruction in the lab, such as when the types of welding joints are best utilized. The teacher may then focus on the acquisition of skills after modeling once for the class. That teacher will then rotate to assist students one-on-one because welders do not typically work in collaboration in the industry. However, teaming may be used in welding so that each student can give the other feedback while the skill is being demonstrated. Of course, lessons in lab safety are paramount to any work beginning and should be continuously reinforced.

In addition to the attainment of technical, industry-specific skills, CTE teachers should also be teaching the 21st-century soft skills—the 4 C's: communication, collaboration, creativity, and critical thinking. Use the welding classroom as an example and think of how these skills could be taught.

In welding, the students can demonstrate communication strategies on the strengths of the welds demonstrated and when the welding joints are best utilized. The students could continue by communicating the weaknesses of the welded joint and how those weaknesses might impact the safety of the structure in which the weld is employed. Further, the student can communicate the ways to improve the welded joint, and students can brainstorm different scenarios in which the integrity of the joint is paramount to safety. This strategy will employ communication, creativity, and critical thinking.

Observations and Feedback

Looney (2011) stated, "Several studies have found that well-designed teacher evaluation systems, aligned with professional learning and development, can contribute to improvements in the quality of teaching and raise student achievement" (p. 440). This statement is packed with instructional supervisory techniques to include observations, feedback, and professional development (PD). Of course, an administrator must start with observations in order to understand the professional learning needs of the staff.

Observations should be conducted with a focus, and teachers should know the instructional foci of the leadership in advance of observations (Westberry, 2020). The focus can shift from one period of time to the next, but these observations should provide valuable information for administration on the PD needed in the building. When the observation data is quantified, that information is a powerful tool for the staff's understanding of the need for PD.

When observing a CTE classroom, administrators need to be aware of the necessary differences. If one expects perfect order, much PD for administrators is needed on CTE classroom expectations. Additionally, an observer must also understand that the formative assessment practice in a CTE classroom will look quite different than those in traditional classrooms. In a traditional classroom, formative assessment practices may include exit tickets or quizzes. However, in a CTE classroom, observation is a strong formative assessment tool.

In fact, several factors will differ. Because the expectations may vary and must include the aforementioned 21st-century learning skills, the observation tool should also differ from a traditional classroom observation tool. With the observation tools, administrators can choose to use the entire instrument or focus on one or two areas for each observation to collect data. Sample elements of the proposed observation tool are broken down so they can be examined.

Instructional feedback can further develop instructional capacities (Mireles-Rios & Becchio, 2018) and improve teacher performance (Donaldson & Papay, 2015). However, this feedback can also have a negative effect if given in the wrong way. The goal is to link feedback to teacher self-efficacy, the belief in one's capabilities to perform a task (Bandura, 1977). Undoubtedly, CTE instructors have confidence and a sense of self-efficacy in performing their craft, the skills that are the foundation of the CTE program. However, performing a job and teaching others to perform that same task requires two different skill sets.

Therefore, observation feedback should be given carefully to highlight the skills present while developing the skills needed. Teachers, when they feel threatened or do not feel their efforts are recognized and appreciated, normally are not open to constructive feedback. However, utilizing feedback from the school as a whole reduces that threat because it conveys the idea that the teacher is not alone. Meaning, the whole school is struggling with questioning techniques, so in this, the CTE teacher is not alone.

The threat of an upcoming feedback conversation can be minimized by providing clear expectations of what information is gathered from an observation that will serve as the basis of an instructional feedback conversation. Tables 12.1–12.4 provide four instructional dimensions along with examples of observable behaviors. While teacher evaluation rubrics are typically standardized for teachers from all content areas, it is important for administrators responsible for conducting CTE observations to understand what evidence to collect and how to best collect it.

Standards and objectives that are explicitly stated, posted, or understood provide learning targets for students. In CTE classes, the learning targets should be related to industry standards specific for the content area as well as the 21st Century Skills that are embedded in the curriculum. Conse-

Table 12.1. Sample CTE observation tool for instructional goals

	Exemplary	Proficient	Emerging	Unsatisfactory
Instructional goals (standards and objectives)	• Objectives are tied to workplace skills and industry credentials • Objectives are connected to previously learned skills and integrated with other content areas (i.e., math, science, etc.) • Objectives are communicated explicitly so that students understand the learning targets • Students are able to effectively articulate what the learning objectives are and integrate it with previous and future learning	• Objectives are tied to workplace skills and industry credentials • Objectives are connected to previously learned skills and integrated with other content areas (i.e., math, science, etc.)	• Some objectives are tied to workplace skills and industry credentials • Some objectives are connected to previously learned skills and integrated with other content areas (i.e., math, science, etc.)	• Objectives are not tied to workplace skills and industry credentials • Objectives are rarely connected to previously learned skills and integrated with other content areas (i.e., math, science, etc.)

quently, the standards and objectives that relate to safety should replicate the industry standards for the specific content area.

For example, automotive safety standards should relate to Occupational Safety and Health Administration (OSHA) General Industry Standards and safety standards for culinary arts should relate to the requirements to obtain the ServSafe Food Handler Industry Credential, which is standard within the hospitality industry and provides food safety training. Successful feedback conversations begin with the focus on the positive of identified behaviors that support this dimension. Using some of the prompts/questions below will help to facilitate a discussion regarding the overall purpose of the lesson.

- What industry skill was the subject of the lesson?
- What is important about this skill?
- How will this skill be used?
- Students knew the industry standard because you . . .
- Students know the expectations because . . .

Effective feedback discussions are beneficial towards the development of teacher practice. "Feedback discussion acts to provide a learning space where vocational teachers and their observers collectively develop vocational practice as teachers in the workplace" (Lahiff, 2015, p. 4). The term *vocational*, of course, is the former term used for CTE. Outcomes from these conversations help transition the teacher to develop their pedagogical approach to teaching.

Specific examples to look for during instructional delivery in a CTE classroom would be the use of modeling workplace behavior, expectations, and skills demonstration. As a specialist, the teacher understands how to demonstrate the connection between the lesson and the CTE content area. Relevant industry equipment should be utilized for demonstrations during the lesson. Teachers should be familiar with the best instructional strategy to use for the specific standard being addressed. One could utilize the questions/prompts below to facilitate discussion within this dimension.

- What could you do to transfer knowledge about . . .
- How could you model . . .
- How can you incorporate the 4C's more effectively?
- What conclusions can you draw about the lesson?
- Students showed 21st Century Skills when they . . .
- You demonstrated effective transition when you . . .
- What do you think you could improve in the lesson?

Naturally, CTE courses are often some of the most engaging classes. Observers of CTE classrooms should be aware that student engagement should directly correlate to the standards, objectives, and pacing for the course. For example, an administrator may walk into a first-level welding class during the first week of school and notice that all of the students are welding individually in the welding booths. It may appear as if all of the students are actively engaged; however, they may not be engaged with the correct content based on pacing and industry standards.

Industry standards require that adequate safety training is conducted with documentation of performance. Based on pacing, students should be engaging in good safety habits prior to practicing welding. When observing CTE classrooms, close attention should be given to determine whether the engagement of students is directly related to the specific standards of the course.

Table 12.2. Sample CTE observation tool for instructional delivery

	Exemplary	Proficient	Emerging	Unsatisfactory
Instructional delivery	• Content is delivered in a clear manner. • Workplace models, examples, and references are used to present content. • Teacher models workplace behavior, expectations, and skills during the lesson. • Teacher presents real life problem-solving opportunities that help develop critical-thinking skills with students.	• Content is mostly delivered in a clear manner. • Workplace models, examples, and references are mostly used to present content. • Teacher models workplace behavior, expectations, and skills during the lesson most of the time.	• Content is sometimes delivered in a clear manner. • Workplace models, examples, and references are sometimes used to present content. • Teacher sometimes models workplace behavior, expectations, and skills during the lesson.	• Content is rarely delivered in a clear manner. • Workplace models, examples, and references are rarely used to present content. • Teacher rarely models workplace behavior, expectations, and skills during the lesson.

Table 12.3. Sample CTE Observation Tool for Student Engagement

	Exemplary	Proficient	Emerging	Unsatisfactory
Engagement	• All students are engaged with the content through activities that are aligned with the standards and standard types (i.e., performance tasks). • Students have autonomy in how they complete instructional activities. • Student activities simulate the work environment related to the content. • Students collaborate to support other students' skill attainment. • Students collaborate on activities/projects that simulate an environment of teams in the workplace.	• Most students are engaged with the content through activities that are aligned with the standards and standard types (i.e., performance tasks). • Students have autonomy in how they complete instructional activities. • Student activities mostly simulate the work environment related to the content. • Students mostly serve as a resource for other students.	• Some students are engaged with the content through activities that are aligned with the standards and standard types (i.e., performance tasks). • Students have some autonomy in how they complete instructional activities. • Student activities sometimes simulate the work environment related to the content. • Some students serve as a resource for other students.	• Students are rarely engaged with the content through activities that are aligned with the standards and standard types (i.e., performance tasks). • Students rarely have autonomy in how they complete instructional activities. • Student activities rarely simulate the work environment related to the content. • Students rarely serve as a resource for other students.

Focus points to provide feedback are shown below.

- Examples where students were engaged in the content at multiple cognitive levels were . . .
- Students were engaged with the teacher and peers throughout the lesson by . . .
- You encouraged students to share their thinking with one another by . . .
- What strategies or structures did you use to encourage participation from all students?

As much as possible, the CTE environment should facilitate learning in a simulated workplace that affords students the opportunity to have an authentic work experience while acquiring 21st Century Skills. During an observation, observers should look for students working collaboratively with teachers and students. In this environment, teachers work collaboratively with students and engage with them to promote communication and critical thinking skills. Procedures that contribute to the efficiency of the simulated workplace environment should be documented. Questions/prompts to facilitate the discussion include the following:

- Your classroom lab resembles a workplace environment by . . .
- Procedures simulate workplace expectations by . . .
- The climate of the environment promotes 21st Century Skills (critical thinking, communication skills, creativity, problem solving collaboration, etc.) by . . .

CTE Programs engage students in learning through *doing*. By students doing and creating, they are utilizing higher levels of thinking. Assessments used throughout the lesson should match the standard being measured. Many of the standards tend to be competency based; therefore, the proper type of assessments, such as a performance task, should be used.

Rubrics, skills checklists, competency checklists, and questioning are some examples of formative assessments that can be used when students are working in a simulated workplace environment. Formative assessments ensure that students are mastering the content as they provide students an opportunity to evaluate their own performance and take responsibility of their learning. Feedback surrounding assessments should provide details about student learning, which should guide instruction. Of course, a rubric for an assessment specific to CTE should be included as well.

The foci for the observations should be shared in advance. By sharing this information, teachers will become more focused on that instructional point, and improvement will occur. Additionally, conveying quantitative

Table 12.4. Sample CTE observation tool on classroom procedures/environment

	Exemplary	Proficient	Emerging	Unsatisfactory
Classroom procedures/ environment	• Routines for operating in a simulated work environment are performed in an efficient manner (i.e., safety inspections/ reviews, lab clean up, changing into uniforms, etc.). • Equipment, tools, and supplies are organized in a way that maximizes productivity and is appropriate for learning. • Industry workplace guidelines are visible and followed (i.e., OSHA Safety rules). • Classroom/Lab environment simulates a safe and efficient workplace. • Students are collaborating to participate and problem solve in authentic workplace activities. • Climate of the classroom promotes collaboration, problem solving, critical thinking, and communication.	• Routines for operating in a simulated work environment are mostly performed in an efficient manner (i.e., safety inspections/ reviews, lab clean up, changing into uniforms, etc.). • Equipment, tools, and supplies are mostly organized in a way that maximizes productivity and is appropriate for learning. • Industry workplace guidelines are visible and mostly followed (i.e., OSHA safety rules). • Classroom/lab environment mostly simulate a safe and efficient workplace.	• Routines for operating in a simulated work environment are sometimes performed in an efficient manner (i.e., safety inspections/ reviews, lab clean up, changing into uniforms, etc.). • Some equipment, tools, and supplies are organized in a way that maximizes productivity and is appropriate for learning. • Industry workplace guidelines are visible but not followed (i.e., OSHA safety rules). • Some of the classroom/lab environment simulate a safe and efficient workplace.	• Routines for operating in a simulated work environment are rarely performed in an efficient manner (i.e., safety inspections/ reviews, lab clean up, changing into uniforms, etc.). • Equipment, tools, and supplies are not organized in a way that maximizes productivity and is appropriate for learning. • Industry workplace guidelines are not visible (i.e., OSHA safety rules). • Classroom/lab environment does not simulate a safe and efficient workplace.

observation data results ensures that the issue, if there is an opportunity for improvement, is *ours* not *yours*. This shift in ownership creates fewer barriers to learning. For this reason, observation data can and should be quantified based on the teaching standards examined and shared with the entire faculty.

CONCLUSION

Observation data and feedback are imperative for teacher growth. CTE teachers are faced with the complexity of planning not only content knowledge but also industry skill and 21st-century workforce skills. Observation forms and feedback should take all of these points into consideration. Additionally, administrators should recognize that most CTE teachers have not been trained in traditional teacher education programs and may not work from the same frame of reference. Furthermore, CTE classrooms are different in design and student expectations. Therefore, feedback for CTE teachers should be structured to help guide them to understanding.

POSTREADING REFLECTIONS/ACTIVITIES

- How can administrators support the infusion of 21st-century workforce skills development in CTE lessons?
- What are the similarities between a marketing classroom and an automotive technology classroom? How are observation expectations the same?
- What are the differences between an English classroom and an EMT classroom? How are observation expectations different?

REFERENCES

Bandura, A. (1977). Self-efficacy: Toward a unifying theory of behavioral change. *Psychological Review, 84*(2), 191–215.

Bradley, B. E. (2014). *Maximizing the use of effective instructional strategies among career and technical education teachers in K–12 education* (Doctoral dissertation, Capella University).

Care, E., Kim, H., Vista, A., & Anderson, K. (2018). *Education system alignment to 21st century skills: Focus on Assessment.* Brookings Institute.

Cheng, A., & Hitt, C. (2018). Hard work and soft skills: The attitudes, abilities, and character of students in career and technical education. American Enterprise Institute.

Donaldson, M. L., & Papay, J. P. (2015). An idea whose time had come: Negotiating teacher evaluation reform in New Haven, Connecticut. *American Journal of Education, 122*(1), 39–70.

Durham, B., & Bragg, D. D. (2019). The contested evolution and future of vocational education in the United States. In *The Wiley Handbook of Vocational Education and Training*, edited by David Guile and Lorna Unwin. Wiley.

Fletcher, E. (2018). Characteristics of career and technical education faculty across institutions of higher education in the United States. *International Journal of Adult Vocational Education and Technology, 9*(1), 42–58.

Korn, F. (2022). No end in sight: Majority of professionals believe employee turnover will increase in 2022. www.kornferry.com/about-us/press/no-end-in-sight

Lahiff, A. (2015). Maximizing vocational teachers' learning: The feedback discussion in the observation of teaching for initial teacher training in further education. *London Review of Education, 13*(1), 3–15.

Lazarus, A. (2013). Soften up: The importance of soft skills for job success. *Physician Executive, 39*, 40–45.

Looney, J. (2011). Developing high-quality teachers: Teacher evaluation for improvement. *European Journal of Education, 46*(4), 440–55.

Mireles-Rios, R., & Becchio, J. A. (2018). The evaluation process, administrator feedback, and teacher self-efficacy. *Journal of School Leadership, 28*(4), 462–87.

National Board for Professional Teaching Standards (2014). Career and Technical Education Standards (2nd Ed.). https://www.nbpts.org/wp-content/uploads/2021/09/EAYA-CTE.pdf

Partnership for 21st Century Skills. (2009). P21 framework and definitions. http://files.eric.ed.gov/fulltext/ED519462.pdf

Rosen, R., Visher, M., & Beal, K. (2018). Career and technical education: Current policy, prominent programs, and evidence. *MDRC*.

Saeger, K. (2017). Career and technical education: The solution for preparing today's youth for college and career. *The CTE Journal, 5*(2), 2–21.

Sturko, P. A., & Gregson, J. A. (2008). Learning and collaboration in professional development for career and technical education teachers: A qualitative multi-case study. *Journal of STEM Teacher Education, 45*(3), 5.

Westberry, L. (2001). One school . . . one step. *Techniques: Connecting Education and Careers, 76*(6), 28–31.

Westberry, L. (2020). *Putting the pieces together: A systems approach to school leadership.* Rowman & Littlefield.

CHAPTER 13

Supervising in a Virtual School Context

Jeana Partin and Mary Lynne Derrington

PREFOCUS GUIDING QUESTIONS

- In what ways does the context of a virtual school change teacher supervision?
- What are online educators' best practices?
- How can teacher performance evaluations be modified for the virtual context?

INTRODUCTION

For some time, educators have been told that the K–12 system designed for the industrial age is inappropriate for the technological era, which supports an outcome-based, personalized education (Zhao & Watterson, 2021). However, change was slow until the COVID-19 pandemic provided an impetus.

Times of crisis can catalyze a slow-to-change bureaucracy, and indeed the pandemic has illustrated that large-scale policy change and educational innovation can happen quickly. As evidenced during the pandemic, opportunities have opened for rethinking both traditional formal-setting education and virtual schools and have continued prompting the reimagining of the educational status quo (Chang-Bacon, 2021).

This chapter expands on the concepts of virtual learning in a K–12 virtual school asked in the prefocus guiding questions. Given the rapidly changing virtual learning environment brought on by the COVID-19 pandemic, virtual school enrollment has increased exponentially, creating a greater need for more school systems and states to develop supervisor observation and feedback expectations.

The first portion of the chapter explains the recent growth of virtual schools and the possible leadership challenges found in a virtual school environment. Documented research on virtual school growth statistics and virtual school leaders' perceptions outlines the basic tenets of a greater understanding of virtual school supervisors' need for specific guidance on how to observe and mentor online educators.

The next section presents the best practice building blocks and definitions specific to virtual learning environments. Since virtual learning occurs in a digital format, the absence of a physical presence presents unique circumstances that should be defined and addressed by virtual educators and supervisors. The primary focus of this chapter provides definitions from key online learning researchers and national and state online evaluation guidelines that support the referenced virtual educator best practices and guidelines, and virtual school supervisor observation and feedback recommendations.

A GROWING ALTERNATIVE TO TRADITIONAL SCHOOLS

Virtual schools are a quickly growing educational alternative to traditional brick-and-mortar schools. Throughout this chapter, a virtual school is defined as a K–12 school that teaches students primarily online through the Internet. Tech experts agree that the digital evolution will continue transforming the way students learn and will result in additional hybrid learning models (Education Reimagined, n.d.; Schwartz et al., 2020; Spectrum Enterprise, 2021).

Increasing numbers of students and their parents have discovered that the virtual learning environment offers flexibility, personalization, and increased time with family (Chang-Bacon, 2021; Gewertz, 2021; Klein, 2021). Another reason for embracing this alternative to traditional schools is leaving a negative school social environment where students experienced bullying or peer pressure (Derrington & Partin, 2022).

In many states, enrollment in online learning increased as an alternative to the often-chaotic quick change from in-person to remote learning during the pandemic (Gewertz, 2021; Richards, 2020; Schwartz et al., 2020). For example, Florida Virtual School's enrollment rose 54 percent for individual online courses and 64 percent for full-time programs in a year. The Pennsylvania Cyber Charter School filled up months before it would have usually started receiving the bulk of new applicants. A virtual charter school in Oklahoma enrolled 1,000 students a day during the pandemic.

In a recent national poll of K–12 parents with at least one child, six in ten said they would likely pursue at-home learning options instead of sending their children back to school; and nearly 30 percent said they would be "very likely" to do so (Page, 2020). In Tennessee, this study's state, the state department public virtual schools' application approvals increased from 17 in 2019 to 57 in 2021. Supporting this trend, a survey of Tennessee's virtual school principals found that 91.67 percent of the respondents expect their enrollment will increase for the 2022–2023 school year.

There are various virtual school models. Some offer a single or limited number of classes online, others are totally online, and still others offer a hybrid model with some days in-person and other days online at home or at another remote location. Despite the variation in scheduling, all virtual schools have a principal who leads and manages the school and supervises teachers in the school.

However, the virtual school's principal is not merely an online version of the brick-and-mortar school's principal. According to Stephenson et al. (2021), "The role of the principal in a virtual setting is not simply the same principal job in a new environment" (p. 23). Consequently, understanding in what ways virtual school leadership and supervision is different from that in the brick-and-mortar school is important to developing and supporting these newly emergent leaders.

VIRTUAL SCHOOLS' LEADERSHIP CHALLENGES

While virtual school principals face many of the same challenges as others, some aspects are distinct (Richardson et al., 2015). Leadership for effective, equitable virtual learning is fairly new. The relatively small knowledge base indicates that leading requires virtual principals who can do the following:

- build a virtual community
- support staff and work alongside teachers in piloting new tech tools and techniques
- protect a student's data with enhanced security tools and practices
- are adaptive, receptive, and responsive to frequent change
- are flexible and nimble in resolving issues requiring a unique response

In addition, like a traditional principal, the virtual school principal serves as the teachers' supervisor with primary responsibility for teachers' professional development and evaluation (Stephenson, 2021).

VIRTUAL TEACHER SUPERVISION AND EVALUATION

Teacher supervision in any context is grounded in the philosophy that "the purpose of supervision should be the enhancement of teachers' pedagogical skills, with the ultimate goal of enhancing student achievement" (Marzano et al., 2011, p. 2). Over the years, developing teaching skills has relied on classroom observations with feedback for instructional improvement as its hallmark (Ponticell, 2016). Such observations can be either informal through such strategies as walk-throughs or formal through the traditional process of teacher evaluation.

Regardless of the approach, teachers value a collaborative process with constructive, clear, and specific feedback they can use to make concrete changes to their teaching practices (Reddy et al., 2017). Evaluation rubrics have been universally used in teacher observations, but they are limited in value to teachers when their specific subject area is not addressed (Lochmiller, 2019).

Moreover, teachers' positive perception of feedback effectiveness is diminished when the evaluation rubric is applied without considering the teaching context (Derrington & Martinez, 2019). Principals also report being constrained by the rubric and consequently adjust when observing subject areas and programs (Derrington & Campbell, 2018).

Although the evaluation and observation process does not provide a clear performance picture, public virtual principals and teachers have the same accountability requirements for teacher evaluation as those in public brick-and-mortar schools. Furthermore, virtual school principals' strategies for supporting teachers' pedagogy may at times be similar to those of brick-and-mortar schools; those strategies include classroom walk-throughs and teacher observations when the teachers are on site (Harrington & DeBruler, 2021). Teacher observation is the cornerstone of performance evaluation even in virtual classrooms.

However, observing virtual teachers is challenging because principals do not see the classroom or students regularly (Stephenson et al., 2021). In addition, other typical supervision tools, such as classroom walk-throughs or conversations in the hallway, do not occur daily, if at all. Yet, teacher evaluation in public schools is required, and constructive formative feedback is needed, particularly in virtual schools (Stephenson et al., 2021). Therefore, the following question is raised: Following an observation, how is individualized, high-quality feedback that enables reflection conducted in a virtual environment?

In a recent survey, 88.3 percent of the principals reported a high need for support in using all the instructional leadership elements, including observation (Westberry et al., 2021). Evaluating virtual teachers can be particularly problematic, as indicated in a recent survey when 66.67 percent of virtual principals responding disagree that the state-mandated evaluation works well (Derrington & Partin, 2022). Moreover, 75 percent of the principals in the same survey stated they regularly modify the teacher evaluation rubric to better suit the virtual context. However, in most virtual school models, teachers are rarely, if ever, present in a classroom working with students.

The principal's challenge of supervising people who are geographically dispersed is underexplored (Richardson et at., 2015). Building relationships with teachers, finding time to observe their teaching, and providing quality feedback may be more difficult in a virtual environment (Harrington & De-Bruler, 2021). In addition, Harrington and DeBruler added that developing trust and support with teachers is critical to teachers' feedback acceptance and lack of time together may diminish trust.

BUILDING A BEST-PRACTICE KNOWLEDGE BASE OF VIRTUAL SCHOOLS' INSTRUCTIONAL LEADERSHIP

Although nascent, there is sufficient research to build best instructional practices in virtual schools. Online learning versus face-to-face learning creates unique situations for teachers and students. The concept of community of inquiry, which includes social presence, teacher presence, sense of community, and construction of knowledge through inquiry and collaboration, represents key attributes of successful online learning platforms and classrooms (Conrad & Donaldson, 2012; Lehman & Conceição, 2010; Palloff & Pratt, 2007).

Therefore, virtual school supervisors' observations and feedback should refer to these important research-based online learning principles. Definitions of online learning's key attributes referred to in the following sections of this chapter are included below (Garrison, 2017).

- *Community of inquiry*—the community of inquiry (COI) is a collaborative-constructivist process designed for online or blended teaching. The learners create a deep and meaningful learning experience through the development of three dimensions or presences: teaching presence, social presence, and cognitive presence.
- *Social presence*—the ability of the learner to identify with the learning community and to perceive their members as "real."
- *Teaching presence*—the binding element in creating the COI is the design, facilitation, and direction of cognitive and social processes to realize meaningful learning.
- *Cognitive presence*—the extent to which learners can construct meaning through sustained reflection and discussion with their peers and the course instructor.
- *Sense of community*—the feeling of being a part of the online community or classroom as if one were present in the real classroom by creating a sense of shared purpose.
- Construction of knowledge—online learners engage in building new knowledge through collaborative online learning tools.

Online educator guidelines using the above-defined theoretical principles are expanded upon in the next section. These guidelines help the novice or advanced virtual school supervisor and online educator better understand virtual learning best practices and enhance feedback opportunities.

ONLINE EDUCATORS' OBSERVATION GUIDELINES

Traditional classroom teachers interact with their supervisors regularly. In contrast, online educators do not have opportunities to interact and develop relationships with their supervisors in the same ways because everyone is not present at the same time. Consequently, principals must create both an online social presence and trust in the online observation environment.

Hence, when observing distance learning, both the observer and teacher can feel more confident with the online observation process if the following observation guidelines are included: using purposefully constructed pre- and postobservation questions related to online learning; gathering evidence and artifacts throughout the planned engagement with the content; and maintaining high expectations for rigorous, standards-aligned instruction. This approach allows for more robust feedback and support for teacher practice and improved student outcomes (TEAM support document, 2022). The observation guidelines are explained later in the chapter.

Preparing for an online class observation, including questions regarding the key components discussed in the following sections, helps the supervisor connect with the teacher, allows for a more comprehensive observation assessment, and provides a rich foundation for the feedback session. The following paragraphs outline the components—teacher planning, instruction, and technology adapted from TEAM (2022), Michigan Virtual (2021), and National Standards for Quality Online Teaching (2019).

The exemplary column in tables 13.1 through 13.4 represents online educator-specific best practices. These more comprehensive guidelines can be referenced in a virtual school's LEA or state-required observation model. Finally, questions are included to help with pre-and postfeedback sessions.

Planning: Technology

Online educators' preparation for instruction is very different from preparing for traditional instruction. One of the first considerations for the online educator is the technology and digital tools used to support student learning. Intentional technology planning enhances the social presence of the students and teachers.

Online learning's use of technology creates a unique environment in terms of a student's safety, security, and accessibility. Creating a sense of

Table 13.1. Planning: Technology

Best Practices	What to look for in a virtual learning classroom:
Planning: Technology	Video conferencing technology (Zoom, MS Teams, Google Meet) is transparent to the learning process and focuses on student-centered learning
	Uses an online, easily accessible SIS and LMS system for students, parents, and administration to access student work, assessment, and grades
	Clear guidelines regarding computer, Internet and application requirements are documented online and sent to parents and students. Facilitates open discussion of the guidelines with students
	All technologies and tools protect student privacy and user data, maintain student information's confidentiality and are current
	Course instructions link to technical support, accessibility policies, and academic support services
	Communication etiquette is well defined; and Internet safety procedures within a getting-started announcement, discussion forum, or other approved method of digital communication are readily available to all students
	Standards of academic integrity are clearly stated

safety helps reinforce the social presence aspect of the online learning environment. An online educator's understanding of the complexities surrounding digital learning tools is vital to creating a sense of safety and security for students and parents.

The supervisor in the feedback session cannot overemphasize the importance of creating cognitive, social, and teaching presence. In a traditional classroom, the presence of the students and teacher is taken for granted. Because the online learning environment lacks the teacher's and students' physical presence, that presence must be compensated for by using online learning tools, technology, and online instructional methods.

The following pre- and postconference questions and evidence collection related to technology planning help guide feedback discussion after an observation:

- What online learning management system (LMS) or other applications do you use to prepare lessons and promote social presence?
- How do you communicate with your students and their parents?
- What types of PD for creating a social presence using technology would you like to receive?
- What online safety protocols do you use to promote student safety and privacy?
- How do you notify students and parents of academic, accessibility, and technical support services?
- How do you communicate and assess issues of academic integrity and online etiquette?

Below is a list of possible instructional online learning tools, and evidence, used in the online learning classroom to assess the use of technology.

Evidence: a) discussion boards, b) email messages to students and parents, c) LMS application, d) SIS application, e) announcements, f) online safety, security, and etiquette instructions; g) LMS and SIS application; h) links to online application's technical support and accessibility options.

Instruction: Presenting Instructional Content and Lesson Structure and Pacing

Online learning promotes cognitive presence—constructing meaning through sustained communication; teacher presence—course design, construction, and facilitation; and social presence—the degree to which a person is perceived as "real" (Palloff & Pratt, 2007). Planning instructional content and pacing lessons are essential in building a community of engagement and promoting cognitive, teacher, and social presence within the online learning environment.

Successful online experiences depend on planned, quality interactions between the instructor and students. Plans should also address equity and diversity considerations to accommodate all students' needs. Furthermore, technology is key to promoting social presence without disrupting the classroom flow. The use of the best practices outlined in table 13.2 helps ensure appropriate instructional content, structure, and pacing.

Table 13.2. Instruction: Presenting instructional content and lesson structure and pacing

Best Practices	What to look for in a virtual learning classroom:
Presenting instructional content and lesson structure and pacing	Creates an online lecture for students with completely clear instructions on how to get started and where to find essential course components Provides a detailed script that checks for understanding, focused standards-based content, and ample opportunity for student engagement and thought Incorporates online assignments aligning with lesson objectives, course content, and assessments Requires timely student response but ensures students a suitable amount of time to complete and submit assignments at their own pace according to their specific needs Students respond to a message board to check for clarity of understanding and meaningful engagement with classmates

The following (a) pre-and postconference questions and (b) evidence collection related to presenting instructional content and lesson structure and pacing help guide the feedback discussion after an observation:

- How do you ensure that all students' voices are included?
- How do you use student feedback to adjust instruction?
- How do you promote equity among learners? Some examples might include various online learning assignments and user-friendly and easy-to-access online tools.
- How do you assist struggling learners?

Below is a list of possible instructional online learning tools and evidence used in the online learning classroom to assess online instruction content and lesson pacing.

Evidence: a) online course syllabus, b) discussion boards or blogs, c) course feedback surveys questions, d) engaging questions or prompts, e) video chats and blogs

Instruction: Questioning/Thinking/Problem Solving

Online, project-based learning—which allows students to reconstruct their knowledge, problem solve, and identify gaps in knowledge—represents a best-practice constructivist approach where students construct or make their own knowledge and the experiences of the learner determine that reality (Elliott et al., 2000). One of the best techniques in online instruction is project-based learning, which allows students to reconstruct their knowledge, problem solve, and identify gaps in knowledge (Tan & Chapman, 2016).

As stated previously, effective learning environments engage learners in socially constructing knowledge requiring interaction and collaboration. The foundation for effective interaction and collaboration is establishing a sense of community among learners. A model of online educators' best practices for project-based learning involves critical thinking, problem solving, and intentional grouping.

In addition, instructor participation throughout the group discussion forum further develops the community of inquiry and promotes the learning objectives (Garrison & Cleveland-Innes, 2005). Online collaboration also provides opportunities for students to participate as global citizens through various digital resources and tools.

Table 13.3: Instruction: Teamwork and Collaboration

Table 13.3. Online educator-specific best practices: What to look for in a virtual learning classroom

Best Practices	What to look for in a virtual learning classroom:
Instruction: Teamwork and collaboration	Assigns online group projects that require teamwork, communication, and collaboration but not always in-person contact Outlines explicit rules for online group work Students create an action plan for group work Checks in periodically with students to help them improve the quality of work Responds to student questions quickly and thoroughly via approved digital communications

The following (a) pre- and postconference questions and (b) evidence collection related to presenting instructional teamwork and collaboration help guide the feedback discussion after an observation:

- What types of projects and other online tools do you use to promote group collaboration?
- How do you provide feedback to encourage critical thinking?
- How do you determine the amount of time needed for adequate group instruction?
- How do you promote community between you and your students?
- How do you use the Internet's resources to promote global citizenship?

Below is a list of possible online learning tools and evidence used in the online learning classroom to assess teamwork and collaboration.

Evidence: a) group projects; b) team discussion boards; c) use of Flipgrid, Google Classroom, Canvas, and so forth.

Table 13.4 Instruction: Academic Feedback and Motivating Students

Table 13.4. Online educator-specific best practices: What to look for in a virtual learning classroom

Best Practices	What to look for in a virtual learning classroom:
Instruction: Academic feedback and motivating students	Expectations for completing the course and calculating grades are clearly defined online for the learner and instructor Consistently provides clear and rigorous written online student feedback on a variety of assignments across instructional styles Always allows appropriate time for students to internalize and clarify feedback online All online assessments align with standards-based, age-appropriate student work and independent/guided practice Always measures student work in more than three ways (e.g., online group projects, experiments, presentations, essays, and short answer/multiple-choice tests)

A successful framework for online learning includes access to technology, guidelines and procedures, requirements, collaborative learning, transformative learning, and appropriate student evaluation of the processes (Palloff & Pratt, 2007). Instructor monitoring of student progress through the online LMS and consistent feedback promote teacher presence. Online educators' timely feedback and grade posting in the school-specified LMS keep the student engaged in the learning process.

The following are (a) pre- and postconference questions and (b) evidence collection related to academic feedback and motivating students to help guide the feedback discussion after an observation:

- How do you prepare lessons to ensure student engagement and adherence to standards?
- How do you monitor students' progress?
- How do you keep students motivated?

Below is a list of possible instructional online learning tools and evidence used in the online learning classroom to assess academic feedback and student motivation.

Evidence: a) grade book, b) feedback on assignments, c) standardized test scores

CONCLUSION

Several studies have examined the problems associated with quickly changing from brick-and-mortar schools to virtual schools during the pandemic. This worldwide change has caused teacher stress, loss of student learning, and parent anger. Nevertheless, evidence indicates that a learning benefit has also resulted.

Evidence indicates that creating quality virtual schools benefits students who might have been disenfranchised in the traditional model or who prefer to work at their own pace. Moreover, parents wishing to participate more in their children's education have found a pathway to such participation. However, these changes have brought the need for new leadership models and considerations for teacher supervision and evaluation.

POSTREADING REFLECTIONS/ACTIVITIES

- How can administrators support online educators through planned observations and constructive feedback?
- What are the key components of constructing a successful online learning environment?
- What are some leadership challenges in virtual schools?

REFERENCES

Chang-Bacon, C. K. (2021). Generation interrupted: Rethinking "students with interrupted formal education" (SIFE) in the wake of a pandemic. *Educational Researcher*, 50(3), 187–96. https://doi.org/10.3102/0013189X21992368

Conrad, R. M., & Donaldson, J. A. (2012). *Continuing to engage the online learner: Activities and resources for creative instruction*. Jossey-Bass.

Derrington, M. L., & Campbell, J. W. (2018). High-stakes teacher evaluation policy: US principals' perspectives and variations in practice. *Teachers and Teaching*, 24(3), 246–62.

Derrington, M. L., & Martinez, J. (2019). Teacher perspectives of evaluation: Five years following reform. *NASSP Bulletin*, 103(1), 32–50. https://doi.org/10.1177/0192636519830770

Derrington, M. L., & Partin, J. (April 2022). *Leaving traditional schools for virtual schools: Exploring pandemic-influenced parent reasons* [Conference presentation]. American Educational Annual Conference. San Diego, CA.

Education Reimagined. (n.d.). www.education-reimagined.org

Elliott, S. N., Kratochwill, T. R., Littlefield Cook, J., & Travers, J. (2000). *Educational psychology: Effective teaching, effective learning* (3rd ed.). McGraw-Hill College.

Garrison, D. R. (2017). *E-learning in the 21st Century: A community of inquiry framework for research and practice* (3rd Edition). Routledge/Taylor and Francis.

Garrison, D. R., & Cleveland-Innes, M. (2005). Facilitating cognitive presence in online learning: Interaction is not enough. *American Journal of Distance Education*, 19(3), 133–48.

Gewertz, C. (2021). Remote learning isn't going away. Will it create separate—and unequal—school systems? *Education Week*, 40(33), 12–13.

Harrington, C., & DeBruler, K. (2021). *Key strategies for engaging students in virtual learning environments*. Michigan Virtual University. https://michiganvirtual.org/research/publications/key-strategies-for-supporting-teachers/

Klein, A. (2021, January 6). We love virtual learning: Students, parents explain why. *Education Week*, 40(17), 8–9.

Lehman, R. M., & Conceição, Simone C. O. (2010). *Creating a sense of presence in online teaching*. Jossey-Bass.

Lochmiller, C. (2019). Credibility in instructional supervision: A catalyst for differentiated supervision. In M. L. Derrington & J. Brandon (Eds.), *Differentiated teacher evaluation and professional learning: Policies and practices for promoting career growth* (pp. 83–105). Palgrave Macmillan.

Marzano, R., Frontier, T., & Livingston, D. (2011). *Effective supervision: Supporting the art and science of teaching*. ASCD.

Michigan Virtual. (2021). *Administrator guide to online learning*. https://michiganvirtual.org/resources/guides/admin-guide/

National Standards for Quality Online Teaching (2019). *Virtual Learning Alliance*. https://www.nsqol.org/

Page, S. (2020, May 27). Back to school? 1 in 5 teachers are unlikely to return to reopened classrooms this fall, poll says. *USA Today*. https://www.usatoday.com/story/news/education/2020/05/26/coronavirus-schools-teachers-poll-ipsos-parents-fall-online/5254729002/

Palloff, R. M., & Pratt, K. (2007). *Building online learning communities: Effective strategies for the virtual classroom* (2nd ed.) [Kindle]. Jossey-Bass, A Wiley Imprint.

Ponticell, J. A. (2016). A retrospective look at data embedded in instructional supervision—Data are not the enemy. In J. Glanz and S. J. Zepeda (Eds.), *Supervision: New perspectives for theory and practice* (pp. 163–86). Rowman & Littlefield.

Reddy, L. A., Dudek, C. M., Peters, S., Alperin, A., Kettler, R. J., & Kurz, A. (2017). Teachers' and school administrators' attitudes and beliefs of teacher evaluation: A preliminary investigation of high poverty school districts. *Educational Assessment, Evaluation, and Accountability, 30*(1), 47–70.

Richards, E. (2020, April 29). What schools will look like when they reopen: Scheduled days home, more online learning, lots of hand-washing. *USA Today.* https://www.usatoday.com/story/news/education/2020/04/29/coronavirus-schools-reopen-online-homeschool/3031945001/

Richardson, J. W., LaFrance, J., & Beck, D. (2015). Challenges of virtual school leadership. *American Journal of Distance Education, 29*(1), 18–29.

Schwartz, H. L., Grant, D., Diliberti, M., Hunter, G., & Setodji, C. M. (2020). Remote learning is here to stay: Results from the first American school district panel survey. *Creative Commons Attribution 4.0.* https://www.rand.org/pubs/research_reports/RRA956-1.html.

Spectrum Enterprise. (2021). Predicting the future of digital learning: Leading EdTech experts look at what's ahead for K12 instruction. https://www.eschoolnews.com/resource-library/predicting-the-future-of-digital-learning/

Stephenson, S. P., Hardy, A., Seylar, J., Wayman, J., Peters, V., Beylin, M., & Roschelle, J. (2021). *Principal leadership in a virtual environment.* Wallace.

Tan, J., & Chapman, A. (2016). *Project-based learning for academically-able students: Hwa Chong Institution in Singapore.* Sense Publishers. https://doi.org/10.1007/978-94-6300-

The Tennessee Educator Acceleration Model (TEAM). (2022). https://team-tn.org/Teacher Evaluation | TEAM-TN

Westberry, L., Hornor, T., & Murray, K. (2021). The need of the virtual principal amid the pandemic. *International Journal of Education Policy and Leadership, 17*(10). https://doi.org/10.22230/ijepl.2021v17n10a1139

Zhao, Y., & Watterston, J. (2021). The changes we need: Education post COVID-19. *Journal of Educational Change, 22*(1), 3–12. https://doi-org.utk.idm.oclc.org/10.1007/s10833-021-09417-3

Themes and Future Directions

Feedback is evaluative information given by supervisors to teachers indicating what can be done to grow and improve. Believing that feedback is a key component of supervision, this book begins with a wide-angle lens of teacher supervision and ends with a telescopic view of providing feedback to teachers in selected content and program areas.

We asked how supervisors become knowledgeable in using content-specific pedagogy to engage in feedback with teachers in informed and credible ways. The authors of this book responded with examples that will be useful to incorporate into both principal preservice and in-service programs. In addition, authors provided observation and feedback tools for supervisors to use in observations of programs and academic domains.

Read in its entirety, the authors provide viable and solid ideas for learning nuances of specific content and program areas. They believe that supervisors who dedicate time can take a big step forward in understanding by learning specific standards, connecting with professional organizations' resources, and seeking published observation criteria relevant to each program or academic subject. Furthermore, a review of the chapters indicates that our authors are united by a set of common beliefs or perspectives.

First, a supervisor's belief shapes the way supervision is approached and feedback is delivered. Teachers can be viewed as either subordinates or equals in the improvement cycle of classroom observation feedback. Evaluative feedback can be transmitted from a deficit or remediation perspective or an assets or growth perspective.

Second, the authors believe in placing teachers in control of their own learning as a powerful way to encourage change and improvement. A key component is to understand that communication is not one-way but that the teacher plays an important role as the receiver of feedback. Therefore, feedback must be responsive to each teacher's unique context.

A third perspective is that consideration of the teacher is paramount in a feedback conference. Specifically, a supervisor's knowledge of the academic subject taught or the teacher's program builds receptivity to improvement. Supervisors who understand course content and programs are more credible and consequently teachers are more accepting of performance feedback.

Fourth, an evaluation rubric used as a checklist rates teacher behavior but does not differentiate for the classroom context or for teachers' professional growth needs. However, a required evaluation rubric can be enhanced by adding selected subject or program indicators. The observer can thereby see the teacher in the context of the lesson, students, and curriculum instead of simply fitting the teacher to a form.

Lastly, a theme across this book's chapters is that providing valuable feedback requires a growth mindset—that is, supervisors who come from a humanistic orientation and put each teacher's needs at the center of communication. This perspective raises the question of whether a growth mindset is teachable or reachable for all current and aspiring school supervisors. Embracing a humanistic approach to supervision requires courage for school leaders to incorporate formative growth approaches in a reductionist rating system.

This book provides productive lines of research inquiry and avenues for supervisory professional development. For example, questions such as the following focus on feedback relationships and training:

- Does a supervisor learn effective and differentiated feedback in university preparation courses and school district professional development programs?
- Is there a relationship between supervisor-perceived credible feedback and a human resource orientation?
- Has research favored supervisory sending of feedback over the importance of the attributes of the feedback receivers?
- In what ways might teachers be part of the two-way feedback conversations? Are they prepared to be an effective part of a growth conversation?
- Are states prioritizing growth and formative approaches in teacher evaluation policies over uniform rating systems?

As editors, we were honored to work with this outstanding group of authors. We deeply appreciate the time they invested to make this book a reality. Collectively, we will continue working on strategies for providing effective and actionable feedback.

We ask that scholars add to the dialogue and research on feedback. We hope that course instructors will use this book in its entirety or as selected chapters. We encourage practitioners to adopt this book's strategies and share applications in practice with colleagues. In these ways, we will continue developing effective feedback practices promoting teacher growth and improvement.

Index

action research, 83, 128
advice networks, 17, 19
andragogy, 24, 26
assessment, 18, 23, 26–29, 44, 51, 65–66, 72, 82, 91, 100, 109, 126–29, 137–38, 140–43, 145, 151, 154–55, 159, 164, 167, 172, 183–84, 186
autonomy, 24–25, 39, 54–55, 59, 67, 171

balanced approach, 49–54, 57–59
best practices, 8, 16, 35–36, 67, 92, 123, 137, 149–50, 155–57, 159, 177–78, 182–86
   check in/out, 40, 42–43
   co-teaching, 154
   eight practices, in STEM, 111
   project-based learning, 154, 185
   promising strategies, 12, 17, 19–20
   walkthroughs, 30, 78, 120, 180
Burkins, Jan, 68

career and technical education, 163–74
   college and career, 163
classroom observation tools, 125
   checklists, 108, 126–27, 130, 172
   rubrics, 39, 41, 108, 111, 116–17, 126–27, 141, 144–45, 168, 172, 180

coaching, 7, 17–19, 26, 29–30, 35–36, 51, 66, 113, 115–16, 129, 143, 154
   instructional coaches, 30, 40, 43–44, 64
   literacy coach, 123, 129–31
collaboration, 17–18, 36, 38–39, 64, 70–73, 117, 142, 145, 154, 157, 165–66, 172, 181, 185–86
collective teacher efficacy, 64, 68–69, 71–72
communication, 11, 24, 52, 102, 109, 117–18, 144, 154, 157, 165–66, 172–73, 183–84, 186, 191–92
community learning exchange, 82
constructivism, 14, 181, 185
content knowledge, 13, 19, 39, 107–10, 116, 126–27, 136, 139, 141, 165, 174
   leadership content knowledge, 108, 110, 136
   pedagogical content knowledge, 13, 19, 107, 126–27
content-neutral practices, 107, 109, 117
context variables, 50, 54, 59
COVID-19, 25, 43, 63, 130, 177
critical colleagues, 81
critical thinking, 92–93, 95, 99, 152, 157, 165–66, 172–73, 185–86

culturally responsive
  classroom practices, 91, 95
  instruction, 76–77, 83–85, 89, 91, 93–94
  markers, 91
  supervision, 75–86
  teaching, 75, 79, 90, 93, 94

data collection, 27, 51, 83
developmental
  approach, 35–37, 43–44
  attunement, 37
  diversity, 43
  lens, 35, 37, 44
differentiation
  learning, 152
  pull-out, 153–54, 158
  self-contained, 153–54, 159
diversity, 43, 75, 77, 84, 113, 159, 184

early childhood education, 138, 141
equity, 75, 77–79, 82–85, 163, 184–85
  equity gap, 163
  instruction, 82, 83, 85
  marginalization, 80, 84–85, 89–90, 94, 102, 118, 164
  minoritized, 84, 90
  positionality, 77, 86
  privilege, 75, 77, 78
evaluative, 12, 23, 25–26, 29, 30, 32, 42, 119, 129, 145
  non-evaluative, 23, 25–26, 29, 30, 32

feedback
  actionable, 36, 91–92, 94–95, 98–103, 107–09, 111, 117, 157, 192
  challenges, 36–37
  conversations, 42, 51–53, 62, 169, 192
  cycle, 63, 65–69, 72, 74, 93
  delayed, 26, 28, 32
  differentiated, 35–36, 42
  effective, 23–24, 26, 68, 127, 131, 136, 156, 169
  evaluative, 26, 29, 32, 129
  focused, 64, 135
  immediate, 28, 32
  indirect, 30
  instructional, 63, 65–68, 72, 74, 167–68
  non-evaluative, 25, 26, 29
  observation, 65, 141, 167
  styles, 38
  timely, 64, 187
formal observation tools, 126
Framework for Teaching, 26–27, 126

Gifted and Talented, 149–60

Hattie, John, 68
high stakes testing, 65
holding environment, 40
human resource
  approach, 49–50, 59
  orientation, 49–60, 62
hybrid learning model, 178

impact cycle, 66–67
inclusion 37, 75–76, 77, 79, 81–82
  classroom, 159
  learning, 81–82
instruction
  effectiveness, 64, 68–69, 71, 73
  feedback cycle, 63, 66–68, 72, 74
  improvement, 11, 17, 65, 68, 71, 76–77, 83, 137, 180
  mismatch, 137
  purpose, 14, 15
  rounds, 30, 31
instructional leadership, 71, 85, 180–81
instructional supervision, 75–79, 81, 83–86, 164

Knight, Jim, 68

learning goal orientation, 50, 58–60
legislation, 50, 54, 56, 59
  teacher supervision, 56, 59
lesson plans, 15, 93
literacy, 123–33, 143–44

mathematics, 26, 107–21
mentoring, 17, 165

Index

National Board Certification, 18, 65, 72

observation
    expectations, 174
    guidelines, 182
    mini-observations, 83
    observer knowledge, 156
    tools, 83, 125–27, 131, 156, 159, 167–68, 170–71, 173

personalized education, 177
postholing, 109
    mathematics, 111
    science, 110
professional
    development, 17, 19, 67–68, 71–72, 79, 84, 91, 128, 131, 138, 179
    growth, 29, 51, 65, 131, 159
    PLC, 18, 36, 128–30

reflection
    practitioners, 13, 66
    prompts, 89, 93, 95, 98–103
    reflection, 23, 26–28, 32, 41–42, 65, 69–70, 80–81, 83, 89, 93, 95, 108, 110, 119, 159, 166, 180–81, 197
    reflective, 13, 39, 41, 64–66, 76, 80–83, 89, 91, 93–95, 98–103, 127
relationships, 12, 16, 19, 23, 38–39, 41, 67, 72, 80, 91, 103, 112, 138–40, 181–82, 192
routines, 14, 20, 102, 130, 141–42, 173

school improvement plan, 95
school board, 54–55, 59–60
science, 107, 111, 114–20, 123–26, 145, 168
secondary schools, 50–54, 56, 58
self-
    assessment, 28, 151
    awareness, 81, 109
    efficacy, 24–25, 68, 71–72, 167
    reflective, 80–81, 127
sociocultural, 75–78, 81, 83–85, 93, 140

strategic
    human resource management, 49
    human resource orientation, 51
    orientation, 49, 59
    planning, 51–53, 59
structural approach, 50
student
    achievement, 12, 17, 63–64, 126–27, 166, 180
    learning, 14, 18–19, 23, 63–65, 69–73, 82, 84, 89, 100, 108–09, 114, 124, 128, 138, 142, 144, 172, 182, 187
summative evaluation, 51, 54, 56, 74
supervision behavior continuum, 80

Taylor, Frederick, 19
teacher
    advice networks, 17, 19
    attrition, 24–25
    collaboration, 18, 64, 71
    efficacy, 64, 68–69, 71–72
    evaluation, 26, 65, 74, 117, 136–37, 141, 145, 158, 164, 166, 168, 180
    knowledge, 12–13
    learning, 12–14, 17, 19, 70, 115, 144
    learning approach, 12–13
    practice, 23, 25, 64, 108, 169, 182
    preparation programs, 71, 73
    retention, 24–25, 164
    rounds, 30–31
    supervision, 49–60, 179, 187
    wellbeing, 50, 56–60
technology, 73, 83, 115, 117, 123, 130–31, 139, 142, 144, 158, 163, 174, 182–84, 187
theory
    adult learning, 24
    theory, 11–12, 19, 23–24, 36–38
Thorndike, Edward L., 1
trust, 16, 23–24, 26, 28, 31, 68, 72, 83, 108, 181–82

unilateral approach, 52–53

video analysis, 63–74
virtual
   community, 179
   online learning environment, 183–84, 187
   quality online teaching, 182
   social media, 81–82, 131
visible learning, 66, 68, 70

ways of knowing
   instrumental, 38
   self-authoring, 39
   self-transforming, 40
   socializing, 39

Yaris, Kim, 68

About the Contributors

Mrs. Sonya Addison-Stewart currently serves as the director of career and technical education in the Berkeley County School District in South Carolina. Prior to this role, she worked as a CTE coordinator in the same district. In total, she has served in CTE for 27 years.

Dr. Monica Anthony is assistant professor of curriculum and instruction at Georgia Gwinnett College. Her research in mathematics education includes preservice middle grades teachers' curriculum use and the influence of productive struggle on the self-efficacy of preservice elementary teachers.

Mark A. Bloom, PhD, is professor of biology and science education at Dallas Baptist University in Dallas, Texas. His research focuses on the intersection of science and religion and investigating best approaches for teaching religiously sensitive socio-scientific issues.

Jessica Blum-DeStefano is a faculty member in the leadership programs at Bank Street Graduate School of Education. Her teaching, scholarship, and approach to leadership foreground the power of growth and interconnection—especially as they relate to individual perspective transformation, authentic collaboration, and capacity building systemwide.

Sarah A. Caroleo is a PhD student exploring teacher development and gifted education policy within Johns Hopkins' School of Education. Having served as both a classroom teacher and a gifted resource specialist, she is passionate about equipping and supporting teachers who instruct students with potential and high-ability learners.

Kimberley L. Chandler, PhD, is the senior program officer/curriculum design, Online Programs for the Center for Talented Youth at Johns Hopkins University in Baltimore, Maryland. Her professional background includes teaching gifted students in a variety of settings, serving as a central office administrator of school district enrichment programs, and providing professional development training for teachers and administrators nationally and internationally.

Dr. Dwayne Ray Cormier is an assistant professor and Urban Education and Family iCubed Research Core Member at Virginia Commonwealth University in the School of Education in the Department of Foundations of Education. Dr. Cormier examines educational sociocultural gaps related to minoritized, marginalized, and otherized students within U.S. preK–12 schools.

Mary Lynne Derrington is an associate professor in Educational Leadership and Policy Studies at the University of Tennessee. She has served as a principal and a superintendent. Her research publication topics include teacher evaluation, policy implementation, and aspiring female superintendents. Her current research focus is leadership of virtual schools.

Geert Devos, PhD, is a full professor in the field of educational administration at the Department of Educational Studies, Ghent University (Belgium). He leads the Bellon research center for school leadership and educational policy. His current research areas include educational leadership, school improvement, and educational policy.

Dr. Janice A. Dole is currently senior research fellow at the Center for the School of the Future, Utah State University. She is the author of research articles, book chapters, and books related to comprehension instruction, professional development, and school reform in reading.

Ellie Drago-Severson, professor of education leadership and adult learning and leadership at Teachers College, Columbia University, is a developmental psychologist and internationally certified immunity to change coach who teaches, researches, and consults with schools, districts, leaders, coaches, and teachers on teaming, self-growth, lifting leadership, and leadership development domestically and internationally.

Colleen Moore Eccles is a nationally board-certified teacher in early adolescence social studies and a mentor teacher supporting novice teachers in Prince George's County Public Schools in Maryland. Her professional interests include coaching novice educators in disciplinary literacy, modeling instructional technology, and sharing strategies for cultivating student voice and civic agency.

Dr. Parker C. Fawson is the Emma Eccles Jones Endowed Chair of Early Education and professor in teacher education and leadership and the director of the Center for the School of the Future at Utah State University. He has authored and coauthored many refereed research reports, book chapters, and professional articles on early reading, reading motivation, and at-risk readers.

Keri M. Guilbault, Ed.D., is an assistant professor and director of the graduate programs in gifted education at Johns Hopkins University. She has worked as a district supervisor of gifted and talented programs, as an instructional coach, and as a teacher of the gifted.

Wyatt Hall is an assistant professor in curriculum and instruction at Georgia Gwinnett College, and a former elementary ESOL teacher. His research includes preservice language teachers' relationships with their mentors during their internships and preservice teachers' integration of their multilingual learners' funds of knowledge into instruction.

Helen M. Hazi is a professor emerita of educational leadership at West Virginia University and has been a teacher, a supervisor of curriculum and instruction, and an expert witness. She writes about legal issues that have consequence for teacher evaluation and instructional supervision.

Jo Beth Jimerson, PhD, is associate professor of educational leadership at Texas Christian University. Prior to her current work with aspiring school leaders, she served for 13 years in Texas public schools as a teacher, assistant principal, and principal. Her research focuses on educational data use, instructional leadership, and the principalship.

Valerie Johnson is the proud principal of Dunbar Magnet Middle School and has been a school principal for six years. After achieving national board certification in 2011, Dr. Johnson learned the importance of ensuring that both teaching and learning occur in all classrooms through reflection of the video analysis process.

Michael W. Krell is a doctoral student at the Center for Mathematics Education, University of Maryland, College Park, where he has supervised secondary mathematics teacher candidates. He is a former STEM teacher and mathematics department chair. His research centers on how multilingual learners participate in classroom mathematical discourse.

About the Contributors

Alyson L. Lavigne, PhD, in an associate professor of instructional leadership at Utah State University. Using her training as an educational psychologist and classroom researcher, Dr. Lavigne examines teacher retention, teachers' beliefs, teacher supervision and evaluation, and culturally and linguistically minoritized students' experiences.

Dr. Ian M. Mette is an associate professor of educational leadership at the University of Maine. His research interests include teacher supervision and evaluation, school reform, and bridging the gap between research and practice to inform and support school improvement efforts.

Dr. Maria Boeke Mongillo is an associate professor in the educational leadership and instructional technology department at Central Connecticut State University. Her research interests and publications include topics of leadership for early childhood education, teacher evaluation systems, disciplinary literacy, and teacher self-efficacy.

Benterah C. Morton (he/him) is an assistant professor of educational leadership at University of South Alabama. His research examines the role leaders play in meeting the needs of diverse populations. He explores this topic by examining mentoring practices and programs, leadership training, and implementation of curriculum and instruction.

Dr. Yanira Oliveras-Ortiz is an associate professor and the assistant director of the School of Education at The University of Texas at Tyler. She has spent 20 years in K–12 education where she served as a teacher, curriculum coordinator, and school principal. Her research agenda and service focuses on the advancement of instructional leadership and supervisors in Belize.

Jeana Partin is a principal of a private hybrid school and a PhD student and graduate research assistant in educational leadership and policy studies at the University of Tennessee, Knoxville. She researches virtual school leadership, character and values in principal preparation programs, rural school networks, and principals' use of mindfulness in decision making.

Sarah Quebec Fuentes is a professor in mathematics education at Texas Christian University, and a former middle and high school mathematics teacher. Her research focuses on classroom discourse, instructional leadership, preservice teacher education, teacher knowledge, educative curriculum materials, teacher self-efficacy, collaboration, and developing fraction sense.

Dr. D. Ray Reutzel is the author of 237 published research reports, articles, books, book chapters, and monographs. He has received more than 17 million dollars in extramural funding. He is the past editor of *Literacy Research and Instruction*, and *The Reading Teacher*. He is the current executive editor of the *Journal of Educational Research*.

Melissa Tuytens, PhD, is an assistant professor at the Department of Educational Studies, Ghent University (Belgium). Her research interests are situated in the field of personnel policy within schools, school leadership, and school policy in general.

Eva Vekeman, PhD, is a postdoctoral researcher at the Department of Educational Studies, Ghent University (Belgium). Her research interests are situated in the field of human resource management for new and experienced teachers in primary and secondary education, the role of school principals in implementing HR practices and its effects on teachers' outcomes.

Dr. Lee Westberry is an assistant professor of educational leadership in the Zucker Family School of Education at The Citadel Military College in Charleston, South Carolina, and prior school administrator at the middle school, high school, and district levels. Recent publications include *Putting the Pieces Together: A Systems Approach to School Leadership*, and *The Virtual Principal: The Many Facets of the Demanding Role*.

Dr. Kristine Reed Woleck is the principal of East Elementary School, a K–4 public school in New Canaan, Connecticut, and a former early childhood and elementary classroom teacher, instructional coach, and mathematics curriculum coordinator. In addition to mathematics instructional coaching publications, Dr. Woleck has facilitated research, development, and implementation of teacher supervision and evaluation systems in her own district for the past 10 years.

Maika Yeigh is an associate professor at Portland State University in Portland, Oregon. She mentors secondary-focused preservice teachers in a graduate licensure program. The heart of her work is mentoring emerging teachers, as well as their university supervisors.

www.ingramcontent.com/pod-product-compliance
Lightning Source LLC
Chambersburg PA
CBHW022012300426

44117CB00005B/154